365 Days of Thanksgiving

"A Spiritual Journey Toward Thankfulness"

Trease Sears

ISBN-13: 978-0692820599
ISBN-10-0692820590

Printed in the United States of America

Ms. Helen!
Thank you for your
support! May the Lord
always bless you!

17

DEDICATION

365 Days of Thanksgiving is dedicated to all those who have been or are currently dealing with depression or even just having a hard time. I encourage you to talk to someone, don't allow it to overtake you. Focus on the things that you can control and find something to be thankful for daily.

ACKNOWLEDGMENTS

First and foremost I thank my God for bringing me through one of the darkest times in my life, especially when I was angry with Him. I thank Him for His loving kindness that surrounded me. When I was too weak to press my way through, He carried me.

To my husband, the last seventeen years have been the most amazing (even when we were going through). Thank you for being everything for me that God desired you to be.

To my children, you each hold a very special place in my heart. I know it seems as if I am hard on you all most of the time but my prayer is that you will understand in due time.

To my mom, dad, siblings, grandparents, nieces, nephews, aunts, uncles, cousins and really close friends, I thank you for your love and continued support.

To all of my many friends, church family, co-workers, Facebook friends, Twitter, LinkedIn, Instagram followers, thank you for being a blessing in my life. Our paths crossing has not been in vain.

.

INTRODUCTION

Rising from Darkness

It was New Year's Eve 2012. We were excited for our evening plans. We had planned to attend the 8pm church service, prior to fellowshipping with our friends. We were invited to two family gatherings and we were geared up to make it happen. Normally, with five children in the house, there was always some type of problem, dispute, or concern. However, this day was different. As we prepared for service the house was quiet and everyone was getting along. There were no signs of chaos and I was happy for the moment.

We arrived at the service, made our rounds, spoke to and loved on our church family until it was time for the service to start. The Worship went forth. People praised God for the things He had done, the doors He had opened and closed, and the ways He had made. Our hearts were being tilled to receive a mighty Word from the Lord; a Word that would catapult us into our new season, our destiny and for some an even deeper relationship with the Father, Son, and the Holy Spirit. 2012 had been a pretty good year and I was ready to experience what the Father had in store for 2013. As the preacher took his place at the pulpit, something began to happen. His words started out so strong, crisp and clear, but after a moment, they faded into the background. I faintly heard him. The room increased in size. I was in a room packed with at least 2,000 people, but it was as if I were alone. All of a sudden, heaviness and darkness surrounded me. I thought about 2012. My mind was restricted; nothing came to my remembrance. *"There has to something…focus,"* I thought to myself. After a few moments, still nothing. I couldn't break free. *What was happening? I had*

1

never experienced this before. I heard a voice say, "All you wanted was to have another child and He didn't allow it. His Word even says, "be fruitful and multiply." "You have given so much time to the work of His kingdom and He couldn't give you this one little desire, after He made you think that He would."

In March 2011, I was at the Sacred Dance Institute Spiritual Intensive in Indianapolis. Mother D. approached me and asked if she could speak with me. I excitedly said, "Yes!" It was always an honor to sit at the feet of this mighty woman of God. She was so full of faith and wisdom. She asked if we could go to a more private area and we did. "You and your husband are expecting something great from the Lord, is that right?" "Yes!" I said. *Who isn't expecting something great from the Father,* I thought. The next words to proceed from her mouth caused my knees to buckle. "A baby," she said. Down I went, in worship. I cried out, "Lord, You do hear our prayers. You have used Your servant to let me know that You do hear us." We had never shared this desire with anyone but the Lord. She handed me a sheet of paper, on it were scriptures of barren women who had prayed to the Father for a child and He blessed them. She told me that He had her to prepare the document in March of 2010 (the year prior). At the time, she wasn't certain as to why, however, she was obedient. That morning He told her to bring it with her and she did. It was for me.

Had the Lord forsaken me? That's what it felt like. As the service drew to a close, I made the decision, that I wanted to go home. *I won't be any good around people tonight,* I thought. My husband saw that there was something going on with me and decided home was where we needed to be. Once we arrived home, I put on my pajamas, got in the bed, and pulled the covers over my head. There I lay, in bed, crying. I couldn't stop the tears from flowing. When my husband entered the room, he said, "Babe, what's wrong?" I didn't know what to tell him because I had not a clue. "I don't know." "Why are you crying?" he asked. I gave a simple shrug of the shoulders. *How do I explain this feeling? What was it?* The children knocked on the door. "Come on, let's watch the ball drop," they said. "You want to come and watch with us," my husband asked. "No," I softly responded. He kissed me on my forehead, told me he loved me and exited the room.

For over an hour, I cried, as I lay surrounded by darkness. I was still unable to recall anything that the Lord had done. I was still breathing, but that didn't register. I was too weak-minded to open one of the many journals that I had kept throughout the year. I was weighed down. My heart had turned cold and dark. *Lord, didn't you say that You would give us the desires of our heart?* I believed it with every fiber of my being. I lived this and

2

shared it with others. I even saw the manifestation of such in their lives. *But wait Lord…what about me?*

My mind was dark; I visualized nothing. I focused only on what I lacked; what had not come to pass. I was depressed and had been for quite some time. It had come upon me in such a subtle way that I was able to maneuver through it until it hit me with one final gut punch. So there I lay; lifeless with no desire to go on. I heard my family outside my bedroom having a good time. My husband came back every now and again to check on me. I wasn't ready to join them. *"Lord, where are you?"* I asked. *"Why have you left me? What did I do?"*

Looking back, in all honesty, the truth was I wanted to stay in that place; feeling sorry for myself. Deep down, I was angry and upset with God and I somehow thought staying in darkness would punish Him for not blessing me the way that I desired to be blessed. As I continued to sulk in self-pity, I heard a voice say, "Get up!" *I don't want to get up; I want to stay right here.* Those were the words inscribed on the pages of my mind. Back and forth, like a game of tug-a-war, the battle between my flesh and spirit became intense. After a few moments, which seemed like forever, I finally pulled it together. I got out of bed, washed my face and joined my family in the other room.

As I entered the room, I was greeted with care and concern, warm hugs and smiles. My heart began to melt, like the warmth of the sun touching an icicle, hanging from the edge of a rooftop. I silently watched *Dick Clark's New Year's Rockin' Eve* trying not to wallow in self-pity. The children sang and danced but on the inside, my struggle continued. The battle was fierce. I felt the tears well up like a sink full of running water. *Is this fight even worth it?* I turned my head so that no one could see me wipe my face. I took a deep breath in, held it and then released it. "Thank You Jesus." My heart spoke. All of sudden, I felt comforted. Again, my heart spoke, "Thank You Lord, for you are sovereign. Your ways are not my ways and Your thoughts are not my thoughts." The Holy Spirit reminded me of the Word that God had been sowing in my heart over the past seventeen years. I felt peace. I felt the strength to fight. He lifted my head and I let Him. It was now time for the countdown, glasses in hand, raised to the sky, as we yelled, "5, 4, 3, 2, 1…Happy New Year!" We drank and shared hugs. It had been a long day. It was time for bed and I felt better. I was given another year.

After a peaceful night's rest and a new lease on life, I was still in awe of how God delivered me from depression's grip. I rose early to prepare breakfast for my family. As I cooked, I talked with God. I expressed that

I never wanted to be in that place again, nor did I want anyone that I knew to experience depression. Immediately, my eyes glanced over to an old empty pickle jar on the counter. It was the kind that housed the large whole pickles. As I gazed upon the jar, I received a download from the Spirit. During breakfast, I shared with my husband and children what the Lord had given me. Throughout 2013, anytime the Lord blessed us in any way, we were to write it on a note card and put it in the pickle jar. On New Year's Day, we would eat breakfast and remember what God had done for us the previous year. Everyone was onboard and excited. In addition to blessings in a jar, I was to use my Facebook account as a ministry tool. From day 1 to day 365, I was to post at least one thing that I was thankful to God for. God showed Himself strong in 2013. He allowed my family to make major strides; accomplishing goals and dreams that we never thought imaginable. One of those dreams was the publication of my first book, *The Art of Becoming One: A Spiritual Journey toward Oneness*. Our organization, The Sow One Foundation, Inc. took flight. We developed and implemented various programs to help our youth and communities to become more productive, educated, and empowered to change the world we live in.

Some of you may be wondering if we ever had another child. After seventeen years, no birth control, countless doctor appointments, fertility specialist and being told that everything is in working condition; there are no problems on either end, there is still no baby. I thought that maybe I misinterpreted what God had said. *Ummm…no, He was very clear.* Maybe, we should give up; stop hoping and praying and just move on. *Ummm…no, we trust Him and we believe that it shall come to pass, at its appointed time.* Even if, He decides to do otherwise, in my eyes, He is still worthy.

Although, I haven't had a physical human birth, God birthed in me the movement that you are now reading. *365 Days of Thanksgiving* will touch the lives of those that the Father allows to encounter it. This is more than just scriptures, hash tags, and a journal; this is my life. I pray that you will be inspired as you walk with me through my journey of thanksgiving. Included is a small journal section for you to write what you are thankful for each day. Join the movement. I encourage you to join our Facebook group *365 Days of Thanksgiving* to share your daily messages of thanksgiving and view uplifting messages and encouraging posts from others.

Day 1

Thank you Lord for brand new mercies! Because of the Lord's greatness, we are not consumed, for His compassions never fail. They are new every morning; great is your faithfulness.
#Heissofaithful

The faithful love of the LORD never ends! His mercies never cease.
Lamentations 3:22 NLT

Today, I'm thankful for:

_____

_____

_____

_____

_____

_____

_____

_____

Day 2

Thankful for breath in my body! Lord only *you* can take my breath away, and then breathe into me an unexplainable newness! I won't waste it! In Jesus name...Amen
#Breathonme

The Spirit of God has made me; the breath of the Almighty gives me
life. Job 33:4 NIV

Today, I'm thankful for:

_____

_____

_____

_____

_____

_____

_____

_____

Day 3
Thankful for the activity of limbs moving on purpose. Thank You, Daddy!
#nolongertakingHIMforgranted

But now God has placed the members, each one of them, in the body, just as He desired. **1 Corinthians 12:18 NASB**

Today, I'm thankful for:

_____

_____

_____

_____

_____

_____

_____

_____

Day 4
Thankful that we serve a forgiving God.
#Forgiventoforgive

The Lord our God is merciful and forgiving, even though we have rebelled against Him. **Daniel 9:9 NIV**

Today, I'm thankful for:

_____

_____

_____

_____

_____

_____

_____

_____

Day 5
Thankful for family! They know me and they still Love me.
#familyLOVE

"A new command I give you: Love one another. As I have loved you, so you must love one another." **John 13:34 NIV**

Today, I'm thankful for:

_____

_____

_____

_____

_____

_____

_____

_____

Day 6
Thankful for the rest received! It is very important that you get an adequate amount of rest in order to serve.
#RestinHispresence

The LORD replied, "My Presence will go with you, and I will give you rest." **Exodus 33:14 NIV**

Today, I'm thankful for:

_____

_____

_____

_____

_____

_____

_____

_____

Day 7
Thankful to have a job to come back to this morning! Oh and I don't have
to leave home!
#itsgreattoworkfromhome!

**And give thanks for everything to God the Father in the name of our
Lord Jesus Christ.** Ephesians 5:20 NLT

Today, I'm thankful for:

_____
_____
_____
_____
_____
_____
_____
_____

Day 8
Thankful for the BLOOD! Yes, it still works!
#bloodbought

**But if we walk in the light, as He is in the light, we have fellowship
with one another, and the blood of Jesus, his Son, purifies us from all
sin.** 1 John 1:7 NIV

Today, I'm thankful for:

_____
_____
_____
_____
_____
_____
_____
_____

Day 9
Thankful for the rain (both natural and spiritual)...even though I don't like getting wet or the extra hassle of carrying an umbrella (tests, trials, and the like). I understand that without rain some things won't grow.
#iwanttogrow

***Every good and perfect gift is from above, coming down from the Father of the heavenly lights, who does not change like shifting shadows.* James 1:17 NIV**

Today, I'm thankful for:

_____
_____
_____
_____
_____
_____
_____
_____
_____

Day 10
Thankful for the WORD of GOD. It provides instruction, expectations, promises, consequences and so much more. It can be an effective tool when we use it!
#knowledgewisdom&power

***All Scripture is inspired by God and is useful to teach us what is true and to make us realize what is wrong in our lives. It corrects us when we are wrong and teaches us to do what is right.* 2 Timothy 3:16 NLT**

Today, I'm thankful for:

_____
_____
_____
_____
_____
_____
_____
_____

Day 11
Thankful for PEACE, which surpasses ALL understanding, guarding our heart and mind in Christ Jesus! Out of my years on this earth, last year alone was one that I could have lost my mind, my faith, and my way. BUT GOD! Thank you Lord for keeping me in perfect PEACE.
#PEACE

And the peace of God, which passeth all understanding, shall guard your hearts and your thoughts in Christ Jesus. **Philippians 4:7 KJV**

Today, I'm thankful for:

_____
_____
_____
_____
_____
_____
_____
_____
_____

Day 12
Thankful for God's grace!
#bythegraceofGod

But He gives more grace. Therefore it says, "God opposes the proud, but gives grace to the humble." **James 4:6 ESV**

Today, I'm thankful for:

_____
_____
_____
_____
_____
_____
_____
_____
_____

Day 13

Thankful for God's protection! Sometimes we don't even realize all that He has protected us from...dangers seen and unseen. #Heismyhedgeofprotection

***The LORD will keep you from all harm--He will watch over your life; the LORD will watch over your coming and going both now and forevermore.* Psalm 121:7 NIV**

Today, I'm thankful for:

_____

_____

_____

_____

_____

_____

_____

_____

Day 14

Thankful for my miracle baby. Doctor's said if you lived to be two-years-old, it would be a miracle. They said that if you lived pass two you would be confined to a wheelchair. After more than five surgeries on your brain by the age of fifteen months, you stand before me today nineteen and thriving. Nothing or no one can overrule God's YES! #HappyBirthdayEboni #miraclesandblessings

***To humans belong the plans of the heart, but from the LORD comes the proper answer of the tongue.* Proverbs 16:1 NIV**

Today, I'm thankful for:

_____

_____

_____

_____

_____

_____

_____

_____

Day 15
Thankful for the mind renewing process. Lesson 1- Exercise financial restraint; just because it's on sale, doesn't mean you have to purchase it. #backtothemallIgo

***Throw off your old sinful nature and your former way of life, which is corrupted by lust and deception. Instead, let the Spirit renew your thoughts and attitudes.* Ephesians 4:22-23 NLT**

Today, I'm thankful for:

_____
_____
_____
_____
_____
_____
_____
_____

Day 16
Thankful for God's direction. He wants to order our steps and direct our paths. We have to be willing to listen and move at the appropriate time. #livingtransformed

***Direct me in the path of your commands, for there I find delight.* Psalm 119:35 NIV**

Today, I'm thankful for:

_____
_____
_____
_____
_____
_____
_____
_____

Day 17
Thankful for God's quiet whisper. His small still voice is comforting when you heed it.
#listenforHisvoice

Come, let us bow down in worship, let us kneel before the Lord our Maker; for He is our God and we are the people of His pasture, the flock under his care. Today, if only you would hear His voice. **Psalm 95:6-7 NIV**

Today, I'm thankful for:

_____
_____
_____
_____
_____
_____
_____
_____

Day 18
Thankful for the increase in Faith. When I prayed (years ago) for an increase in Faith, I didn't realize that some issues, circumstances, and test would have to come my way in order to effectively experience the increase. But I made it, and I am trusting God even more. #FAITHinAction

Now faith is the substance of things hoped for, the evidence of things not seen. **Hebrews 11:1 KJV**

Today, I'm thankful for:

_____
_____
_____
_____
_____
_____
_____
_____

Day 19
Thankful that God allowed me to have an earthly father. Parents should not be taken for granted.
#Ilovemydad

Honor your father and your mother, as the LORD your God has commanded you, so that you may live long and that it may go well with you in the land the LORD your God is giving you.
Deuteronomy 5:16 NIV

Today, I'm thankful for:

_____
_____
_____
_____
_____
_____
_____
_____

Day 20
Thankful for the way that He loves us! His love is unconditional.
#HisloveNEVERfails

For God so loved the world that He gave his one and only Son, that whoever believes in Him shall not perish but have eternal life.
John 3:16 NIV

Today, I'm thankful for:

_____
_____
_____
_____
_____
_____
_____
_____

Day 21

Thankful for every opportunity to minister. Lord, I pray that your Glory feels every place! #showusYourGlory

Praise be to his glorious name forever; may the whole earth be filled with his glory. Amen and Amen. Psalm 72:19 NIV

Today, I'm thankful for:

_____

_____

_____

_____

_____

_____

_____

_____

Day 22

Thankful for the discipline that I have received, the lessons learned (from both God and my parents). Those lessons shaped me into who I am today. Don't look at it as punishment; learn from it and be transformed. #beingtransformed

Do not conform to the pattern of this world, but be transformed by the renewing of your mind. Then you will be able to test and approve what God's will is--His good, pleasing, and perfect will. Romans 12:2 NIV

Today, I'm thankful for:

_____

_____

_____

_____

_____

_____

_____

_____

Day 23

Thankful for health. Some of us never think about health issues when we're healthy. To God be the Glory for good health.
#goodhealthgoodliving

***Dear friend, I pray that you may enjoy good health and that all may go well with you, even as your soul is getting along well.*
3 John 1:2 NIV**

Today, I'm thankful for:

_____

_____

_____

_____

_____

_____

_____

_____

Day 24

Thankful for another chance. He didn't have to but He breathed on me today, (and if you're reading this, you have breath as well). Let's make this day worth the very breath God breathes on us! Praise Him!
#Hehasgivenmemanychances

***You have made my life no longer than the width of my hand. My entire lifetime is just a moment to you; at best, each of us is but a breath.* Psalm 39:5 NLT**

Today, I'm thankful for:

_____

_____

_____

_____

_____

_____

_____

_____

Day 25

Thankful for true love, it does cover a multitude of sins. No one can love you like Jesus! His sacrifice for us was extreme. He went the distance! Let's commemorate His love for us by loving others (especially those we find it difficult to love). #GodisLove

Above all, love each other deeply, because love covers over a multitude of sins. 1 Peter 4:8 NIV

Today, I'm thankful for:

_____

_____

_____

_____

_____

_____

_____

_____

Day 26

Thankful for laughter; especially when I laugh so hard that my stomach hurts! #goodmedicine

Our mouths were filled with laughter, our tongues with songs of joy. Then it was said among the nations, "The LORD has done great things for them." Psalm 126:2 NIV

Today, I'm thankful for:

_____

_____

_____

_____

_____

_____

_____

_____

Day 27
Thankful for patience. It's always a good thing to breathe and think before you react! Your delay could be a blessing in disguise.
#thinkfirst

Understand this, my dear brothers and sisters: You must all be quick to listen, slow to speak, and slow to get angry. James 1:19 NLT

Today, I'm thankful for:

_____
_____
_____
_____
_____
_____
_____
_____

Day 28
Thankful for the opportunity to give God more. He wants us to be more loving, kind, patient, more peaceful, and humble.
#Hewantsmore

Therefore, as God's chosen people, holy and dearly loved, clothe yourselves with compassion, kindness, humility, gentleness and patience. Colossians 3:12 NIV

Today, I'm thankful for:

_____
_____
_____
_____
_____
_____
_____
_____

Day 29

Thankful for the wait! Although sometimes waiting is hard (and we don't want to do it), I am learning that I don't want anything from God until He is ready for me to have it.

#Histimingisperfect #nottryingtomessupmyblessing

For the evildoers shall be cut off, but those who wait for the LORD shall inherit the land. Psalm 37:9 ESV

Today, I'm thankful for:

_____

_____

_____

_____

_____

_____

_____

_____

Day 30

Thankful for the ability to gain knowledge. Try to learn something new every day. #knowledgeispower

The fear of the LORD is the beginning of knowledge, but fools despise wisdom and instruction. Proverbs 1:7 NIV

Today, I'm thankful for:

_____

_____

_____

_____

_____

_____

_____

_____

Day 31
Thankful that when I seek the Lord first, He meets my needs.
#Heisaneedmeeter #seekHimwhenyourise

Seek the Kingdom of God above all else, and live righteously, and He will give you everything you need. Matthew 6:33 NLT

Today, I'm thankful for:

_____
_____
_____
_____
_____
_____
_____
_____

Day 32
Thankful for the warmth of the sun (Son).
#thesunisshining

From the rising of the sun to the place where it sets, the name of the LORD is to be praised. Psalm 113:3 NIV

Today, I'm thankful for:

_____
_____
_____
_____
_____
_____
_____
_____

Day 33
Thankful for shelter. Find safety in the Master's arm.
#Hisarmsarestrong

How priceless is your unfailing love, O God! People take refuge in the shadow of your wings. **Psalm 36:7 NIV**

Today, I'm thankful for:

_____

_____

_____

_____

_____

_____

_____

_____

Day 34
Thankful for God's love, even though there are days and times when I don't deserve it. He loves me without conditions and I had to learn to accept that. Life is so much better knowing that I have received the undying Love of Jesus Christ.
#receiveHisLove

Your unfailing love, O LORD, is as vast as the heavens; your faithfulness reaches beyond the clouds. **Psalm 36:5 NLT**

Today, I'm thankful for:

_____

_____

_____

_____

_____

_____

_____

_____

Day 35

Thankful for the freedom to study the Word of God. There are people in some countries who have to sneak to read the Word and the consequences for being caught can be life threatening. So while I have the freedom to do so, I'm going to open the Good Book and be blessed! #theWordisBlessed

Blessed is the one who reads aloud the words of this prophecy, and blessed are those who hear it and take to heart what is written in it, because the time is near. Revelation 1:3 NIV

Today, I'm thankful for:

_____
_____
_____
_____
_____
_____
_____
_____

Day 36

Thankful for positive teachers who teach with compassion. Teachers who help to reiterate my expectations for my children. #teachwithcompassion

When Jesus landed and saw a large crowd, He had compassion on them, because they were like sheep without a shepherd. So He began teaching them many things. Mark 6:34 NIV

Today, I'm thankful for:

_____
_____
_____
_____
_____
_____
_____

Day 37
Thankful for wisdom. It goes a long way. Ask for it; God gives it
generously! #letwisdomguideyou

If any of you lacks wisdom, you should ask God, who gives
generously to all without finding fault, and it will be given to you.
James 1:5 NIV

Today, I'm thankful for:

Day 38
Thankful that You know my beginning and my end; no matter what anyone
says or does. You have the last say so.
#Godknowsbest

Only I can tell you the future before it even happens. Everything I
plan will come to pass, for I do whatever I wish. **Isaiah 46:10 NLT**

Today, I'm thankful for:

Day 39
Thankful for wonderful friends who go the extra mile to make a lady feel special. #wantfriendsbefriendly

"A Friends loves at all times." **Proverbs 17:17a NIV**

Today, I'm thankful for:

_____
_____
_____
_____
_____
_____
_____
_____

Day 40
Thankful for another year! Lord, You have truly blessed me. It is great to have life and have it abundantly.
#abundantlife

You crown the year with your bounty, and your carts overflow with abundance. **Psalm 65:11 NIV**

Today, I'm thankful for:

_____
_____
_____
_____
_____
_____
_____
_____

Day 41

Thankful for being created in His image. I am beautiful, loving, patient, creative and good; and so are you!
#Smooches

Then God said, "Let us make mankind in our image, in our likeness, so that they may rule over the fish in the sea and the birds in the sky, over the livestock and all the wild animals, and over all the creatures that move along the ground." Genesis 1:26 NIV

Today, I'm thankful for:

_____

_____

_____

_____

_____

_____

_____

_____

Day 42

Thankful for food, clothing, and shelter. In today's society we probably know someone who is lacking one, two or all three of these necessities. Pay close attention and help where you can. Let's get on our job saints!
#basicneedsmet

It is a sin to despise one's neighbor, but blessed is the one who is kind to the needy. Proverbs 14:21 NIV

Today, I'm thankful for:

_____

_____

_____

_____

_____

_____

_____

_____

Day 43
Thankful for the dots that God is connecting in my life.
#connectthedots

Many are the plans in a person's heart, but it is the LORD's purpose that prevails. **Proverbs 19:21 NIV**

Today, I'm thankful for:

_____
_____
_____
_____
_____
_____
_____
_____
_____

Day 44
Thankful that through it all, You (God) never left me nor have you forsaken me. Family and friends walked out but You have remained Faithful and True. You are the one constant in my life. You don't falter. Our relationship is not based on what I can do for You but the fact that you loved me enough to give your only begotten son in exchange for my ratchet life! Hallelujah!
#receivingandacceptingHislove

The LORD himself goes before you and will be with you; He will never leave you nor forsake you. Do not be afraid; do not be discouraged. **Deuteronomy 31:8 NIV**

Today, I'm thankful for:

_____
_____
_____
_____
_____
_____
_____
_____

Day 45

Thankful for seeing smiles on my children's faces. They are truly a gift from God! Eboni, Curtisha, Jaylan, Jaykeis, and Makia, I am proud to be called your mom. I love you all!
#rewarded

**Children are a gift from the LORD; they are a reward from Him.
Psalm 127:3 NLT**

Today, I'm thankful for:

_____

_____

_____

_____

_____

_____

_____

_____

_____

Day 46

Thankful for the Holy Spirit. He comforts us and leads us. As long as we follow His leading we don't have to worry about being led in the wrong direction.
#directourpaths

**When the Spirit of truth comes, He will guide you into all the truth, for He will not speak on his own authority, but whatever He hears He will speak, and He will declare to you the things that are to come.
John 16:13 ESV**

Today, I'm thankful for:

_____

_____

_____

_____

_____

_____

_____

_____

_____

Day 47
Thankful for perfect love which casts out *all* fear! Seek Jesus and you will find it. #nofear

There is no fear in love. But perfect love drives out fear, because fear has to do with punishment. The one who fears is not made perfect in love. 1 John 4:18 NIV

Today, I'm thankful for:

_____
_____
_____
_____
_____
_____
_____
_____

Day 48
Thankful for the blessings of the Lord! We are blessed beyond measure because we serve a great God.
#blessedandfavored

From his abundance we have all received one gracious blessing after another. John 1:16 NLT

Today, I'm thankful for:

_____
_____
_____
_____
_____
_____
_____
_____

Day 49

Thankful for the opportunity to be a blessing to others. God wants us to live together in unity; loving, encouraging, and helping one another! Step outside your box today and encourage, help, and love someone! #blessedtobless

How good and pleasant it is when God's people live together in unity! **Psalm 133:1 NIV**

Today, I'm thankful for:

_____

_____

_____

_____

_____

_____

_____

_____

Day 50

Thankful for daily devotional time. God speaks to us and hears our cry. #wecrytoyou

I love the LORD, for He heard my voice; He heard my cry for mercy. Psalm 116:1 NIV

Today, I'm thankful for:

_____

_____

_____

_____

_____

_____

_____

Day 51
Thankful that we serve an all-knowing God! He knows *everything*, even when we don't voice it. To God be the Glory!
#HeknowsitALL

For God watches how people live; He sees everything they do.
Job 34:21 NLT

Today, I'm thankful for:

_____
_____
_____
_____
_____
_____
_____
_____

Day 52
Thankful for the little/big things. Little in size/time but have a big impact: playing a game of UNO with the children, letting them comb my hair, black history nuggets, a scripture memory contest, and more. Slow down, breathe and enjoy the gifts that God gave you! #bewisewithyourtime

Look carefully then how you walk, not as unwise but as wise, making the best use of the time, because the days are evil.
Ephesians 5:15-16 ESV

Today, I'm thankful for:

_____
_____
_____
_____
_____
_____
_____
_____

Day 53

Thankful when the schedule is clear for the evening.
#loungingisgoodsometime!

Return to your rest, my soul, for the LORD has been good to you.
Psalm 116:7 NIV

Today, I'm thankful for:

Day 54

Thankful that even when we don't fully understand all that we may be
facing right now, know that God has your best interest at heart. Help is on
the way! #bestrongandhangon

I lift up my eyes to the mountains-- where does my help come from?
My help comes from the LORD, the Maker of heaven and earth.
Psalm 121:1-2 NIV

Today, I'm thankful for:

Day 55
Thankful for His sustaining power. Lord, we thank you for keeping us in the midst of it all!
#perfectpeace

You will keep in perfect peace those whose minds are steadfast, because they trust in you. Isaiah 26:3 NIV

Today, I'm thankful for:

_____
_____
_____
_____
_____
_____
_____
_____

Day 56
Thankful that He will put a guard over our mouths. Everything we think doesn't have to be said.
#trytooperatewithWisdom

Set a guard over my mouth, LORD; keep watch over the door of my lips. Psalm 141:3 NIV

Today, I'm thankful for:

_____
_____
_____
_____
_____
_____
_____
_____

Day 57

Thankful for the presence of God! Lord I thank You for allowing me to experience Your presence. I am *not* worthy!
#getfullinHispresence

***Thou wilt shew me the path of life: in thy presence is fullness of joy; at thy right hand there are pleasures for evermore.* Psalm 16:11 KJV**

Today, I'm thankful for:

_____

_____

_____

_____

_____

_____

_____

_____

Day 58

Thankful that we are not called to lean to our own understanding because sometimes our understanding is so far from the truth.
#trytofindGodineverything

***Trust in the LORD with all your heart and lean not on your own understanding; in all your ways submit to Him, and He will make your paths straight.* Proverbs 3:5-6 NIV**

Today, I'm thankful for:

_____

_____

_____

_____

_____

_____

_____

_____

Day 59
Thankful for power, love, and a sound mind - all which are gifts from God. Fear can't and will no longer live here.
#tappingintothethingsofGod!

For God hath not given us the spirit of fear; but of power, and of love, and of a sound mind. 2 Timothy 1:7 KJV

Today, I'm thankful for:

_____

_____

_____

_____

_____

_____

_____

_____

Day 60
Thankful for purpose! God has divine plans for our lives. His plans will prosper us and not harm us; and give us hope and a future.
#letswalkinHisplans

"For I know the plans I have for you," declares the LORD, "plans to prosper you and not to harm you, plans to give you hope and a future." Jeremiah 29:11 NIV

Today, I'm thankful for:

_____

_____

_____

_____

_____

_____

_____

_____

Day 61

Thankful that God sees and knows all. If He didn't, I would be a mess. His Spirit definitely keeps me in line!
#theALLknowingGod

***Nothing in all creation is hidden from God's sight. Everything is uncovered and laid bare before the eyes of Him to whom we must give account.* Hebrews 4:13 NIV**

Today, I'm thankful for:

_____

_____

_____

_____

_____

_____

_____

_____

Day 62

Thankful for knowledge. For without it, you will perish.
#getKNOWLEDGE

***My people are destroyed for lack of knowledge. Because you have rejected knowledge, I also will reject you from being My priest. Since you have forgotten the law of your God, I also will forget your children.* Hosea 4:6 NASB**

Today, I'm thankful for:

_____

_____

_____

_____

_____

_____

_____

_____

Day 63
Thankful that I don't have to want for anything. The Master has me
covered. He meets my every need.
#nolack

The LORD is my shepherd; I have all that I need.
Psalm 23:1 NLT

Today, I'm thankful for:

_____

_____

_____

_____

_____

_____

_____

Day 64
Thankful that you are a miracle working God! Lord, we are standing in
need of miracles. In Jesus' name. Amen.
#flow

You are the God of great wonders! You demonstrate your awesome
power among the nations. Psalm 77:14 NLT

Today, I'm thankful for:

_____

_____

_____

_____

_____

_____

_____

Day 65
Thankful for clearer vision. When the pressures of life weigh me down, You lift me up.
#goinghigherinHIM

The LORD opens the eyes of the blind. The LORD lifts up those who are weighed down. The LORD loves the godly.
Psalm 146:8 NLT

Today, I'm thankful for:

_____
_____
_____
_____
_____
_____
_____
_____

Day 66
Thankful for the ability to worship the Lord in dance. Whatever gift(s) He has blessed us with; let's make sure that we are using them to build His Kingdom and not our own selfish motives.
#Hecanseeyou!

Each of you should use whatever gift you have received to serve others, as faithful stewards of God's grace in its various forms.
1 Peter 4:10 NIV

Today, I'm thankful for:

_____
_____
_____
_____
_____
_____
_____
_____

Day 67
Thankful for the overflowing blessings of God! He has it waiting for you.
#milkandhoney

And God is able to bless you abundantly, so that in all things at all times, having all that you need, you will abound in every good work.
2 Corinthians 9:8 NIV

Today, I'm thankful for:

_____

_____

_____

_____

_____

_____

_____

_____

Day 68
Thankful for the small lessons that help us realize we serve a big God.
#Hecan

"Behold, I am the LORD, the God of all flesh; is anything too difficult for Me?" Jeremiah 32:27 NASB

Today, I'm thankful for:

_____

_____

_____

_____

_____

_____

_____

_____

Day 69
Thankful for God tilling the ground of my heart. What kind of ground (heart) did the Word fall on today? It's not enough to be hearers of the Word but we must also be doers.
#applywhatyouhear!

But don't just listen to God's word. You must do what it says. Otherwise, you are only fooling yourselves. **James 1:22 NLT**

Today, I'm thankful for:

_____
_____
_____
_____
_____
_____
_____
_____
_____

Day 70
Thankful for good sense and insight from the Lord. Today will be a great day!
#itwillbewhatyoumakeit

For the LORD gives wisdom; from his mouth come knowledge and understanding. **Proverbs 2:6 NIV**

Today, I'm thankful for:

_____
_____
_____
_____
_____
_____
_____

Day 71
Thankful for great leaders. Whether at home, church, or work, God has allowed me to be in the midst of and learn from some great and humble people.
#celebrategreatleaders

He cared for them with a true heart and led them with skillful hands.
Psalm 78:72 NLT

Today, I'm thankful for:

_____
_____
_____
_____
_____
_____
_____
_____

Day 72
Thankful for the transformation process. It is not an easy process. It can actually be pretty yucky and painful at times, but once the change occurs, the possibilities are limitless! Once transformed you can't go back. Have you ever seen a butterfly become a caterpillar?
#getyourwingsandsoar!

Therefore, if anyone is in Christ, the new creation has come: The old has gone, the new is here! **2 Corinthians 5:17 NIV**

Today, I'm thankful for:

_____
_____
_____
_____
_____
_____
_____
_____

Day 73
Thankful for praying friends. The prayers of the righteous availeth much.
#praywithoutceasing

Confess your faults one to another, and pray one for another, that ye may be healed. The effectual fervent prayer of a righteous man availeth much. James 5:16 KJV

Today, I'm thankful for:

_____
_____
_____
_____
_____
_____
_____
_____

Day 74
Thankful for restoration! You have restored my hope, my determination, my passion, my desire and my soul to do Your will.
#Greatthingsinstore

He restores my soul. He leads me in paths of righteousness for his name's sake. Psalm 23:3 ESV

Today, I'm thankful for:

_____
_____
_____
_____
_____
_____
_____
_____

Day 75
Thankful that one apple seed has the potential to produce many apples.
Sow your seed in good ground. Be fruitful and watch God multiply it!
#beingfruitful

Do not be deceived: God is not mocked, for whatever one sows, that will he also reap. **Galatians 6:7 ESV**

Today, I'm thankful for:

_____
_____
_____
_____
_____
_____
_____
_____

Day 76
Thankful that my hope is in Christ. Even when I see no way out, I trust in
Him.
#myhopeandtrustareinYou

May the God of hope fill you with all joy and peace as you trust in Him, so that you may overflow with hope by the power of the Holy Spirit. **Romans 15:13 NIV**

Today, I'm thankful for:

_____
_____
_____
_____
_____
_____
_____
_____

Day 77
Thankful for the opportunity to go to God on my own behalf. The veil was torn top to bottom when Jesus died. You can talk to Him, too. He's waiting on you. Prayer changes things. Whether it is your situation, or your response to your situation, give Him a try!
#beyondtheveil

With a loud cry, Jesus breathed his last. The curtain of the temple was torn in two from top to bottom. Mark 15:37-38 NIV

Today, I'm thankful for:

_____

_____

_____

_____

_____

_____

_____

_____

Day 78
Thankful for joy unspeakable joy. The joy of the Lord is my strength. Even when all hell is breaking loose, you can still smile and encourage others.
#bestronginHim

The LORD is my strength and my shield; my heart trusts in Him, and He helps me. My heart leaps for joy, and with my song I praise Him. Psalm 28:7 NIV

Today, I'm thankful for:

_____

_____

_____

_____

_____

_____

_____

_____

Day 79
Thankful that our God is REAL! He's not a statue or any other THING.
He is true and living. We can cast all our cares upon Him because He cares
for us.
#TRUTH

Give all your worries and cares to God, for He cares about you.
1 Peter 5:7 NLT

Today, I'm thankful for:

_____
_____
_____
_____
_____
_____
_____
_____

Day 80
Thankful for another opportunity to die today. Killing my own fleshly
desires and submitting to you, Lord. Help me to walk in righteousness for
your namesake. This walk is a day-by-day, hour-by-hour, minute-by-minute
process.
#dietothefleshdaily

***I have been crucified with Christ; and it is no longer I who live, but
Christ lives in me; and the life which I now live in the flesh I live by
faith in the Son of God, who loved me and gave Himself up for me.***
Galatians 2:20 NASB

Today, I'm thankful for:

_____
_____
_____
_____
_____
_____
_____
_____

Day 81

Thankful for love without hypocrisy. God truly does love us and because He loves us we can love others.
#Hisloveistrue

Let love be without hypocrisy. Abhor what is evil; cling to what is good. Romans 12:9 NASB

Today, I'm thankful for:

_____
_____
_____
_____
_____
_____
_____
_____

Day 82

Thankful for self-control. Some people will do or say anything to get you to respond in a negative way. They will try to prove that you are not who you proclaim to be. Walk in the servitude of Christ and let the Father fight your battles. #Godhasit

All those gathered here will know that it is not by sword or spear that the Lord saves; for the battle is the Lord's, and He will give all of you into our hands. 1 Samuel 17:47 NIV

Today, I'm thankful for:

_____
_____
_____
_____
_____
_____
_____
_____

Day 83
Thankful for a "right now" spirit. It is important to move when the Lord says move. #somethingsmoving #somethingschanging

Whether the cloud stayed over the tabernacle for two days or a month or a year, the Israelites would remain in camp and not set out; but when it lifted, they would set out. At the LORD's command they encamped, and at the LORD's command they set out. They obeyed the LORD's order, in accordance with his command through Moses. **Numbers 9:22-23 NIV**

Today, I'm thankful for:

_____
_____
_____
_____
_____
_____
_____
_____

Day 84
Thankful for the Holy Ghost. He sometimes comes in like a whispering wind and other times He comes in mightily! He has life changing power. #don'tcarehowHecomesaslongasHecomes!

Suddenly, there was a sound from heaven like the roaring of a mighty windstorm, and it filled the house where they were sitting. Then, what looked like flames or tongues of fire appeared and settled on each of them. And everyone present was filled with the Holy Spirit and began speaking in other languages, as the Holy Spirit gave them this ability. **Acts 2:2-4 NLT**

Today, I'm thankful for:

_____
_____
_____
_____
_____
_____
_____

Day 85

Thankful for the Holy Ghost ministering through me. Each and every time, He ministers to me. Be open for God to use you and watch Him began to reveal things to you. #listentotheSpirit

When we tell you these things, we do not use words that come from human wisdom. Instead, we speak words given to us by the Spirit, using the Spirit's words to explain spiritual truths. **1 Corinthians 2:13 NLT**

Today, I'm thankful for:

_____
_____
_____
_____
_____
_____
_____
_____

Day 86

Thankful for the Redeemer Jesus Christ. We have been cleared. We are not our own, we were bought with His life.
#redeemedbythebloodoftheLamb
#thebloodstillworks

He is so rich in kindness and grace that He purchased our freedom with the blood of his Son and forgave our sins. **Ephesians 1:7 NLT**

Today, I'm thankful for:

_____
_____
_____
_____
_____
_____
_____
_____

Day 87
Thankful for the gifts of the Spirit. Each one of us have specific gifts to be used for His Kingdom. Do your part so that He is glorified and His Kingdom flourishes.
#whatshouldyoubedoing?

We have different gifts, according to the grace given to each of us. If your gift is prophesying, then prophesy in accordance with your faith; if it is serving, then serve; if it is teaching, then teach; if it is to encourage, then give encouragement; if it is giving, then give generously; if it is to lead, do it diligently; if it is to show mercy, do it cheerfully. **Romans 12:6-8 NIV**

Today, I'm thankful for:

_____
_____
_____
_____
_____
_____
_____
_____

Day 88
Thankful for the sacrifice He made for me. He didn't have to go through it but He did. Hallelujah!
#becauseHedidIdo

But God demonstrates his own love for us in this: While we were still sinners, Christ died for us. **Romans 5:8 NIV**

Today, I'm thankful for:

_____
_____
_____
_____
_____
_____
_____
_____

Day 89

Thankful for the talents God blessed my family with. All the Glory belongs to Him! Use what He gave you to glorify His name.
#donotwasteit

To one He gave five talents, to another two, to another one, to each according to his ability. Then He went away. **Matthew 25:15 ESV**

Today, I'm thankful for:

Day 90

Thankful that God has NOT given us the spirit of Fear. He tells us many times in His Word to, "Fear not."
#releasethefear

So do not fear, for I am with you; do not be dismayed, for I am your God. I will strengthen you and help you; I will uphold you with my righteous right hand. **Isaiah 41:10 NIV**

Today, I'm thankful for:

Day 91
Thankful for the small moments with friends. You all know who you are.
Smooches! #oneofakind #Icallyoufriend

A man that hath friends must shew himself friendly: and there is a friend that sticketh closer than a brother. Proverbs 18:24 KJV

Today, I'm thankful for:

_____

_____

_____

_____

_____

_____

_____

_____

Day 92
Thankful for the wonderful change that has come over me. It is my desire
to please God in all that I do. Won't you join me?
#giveHimGlory!

The mind governed by the flesh is hostile to God; it does not submit to God's law, nor can it do so. Those who are in the realm of the flesh cannot please God. Romans 8:7-8 NIV

Today, I'm thankful for:

_____

_____

_____

_____

_____

_____

_____

_____

Day 93

Thankful that God has given us the power to resist the enemy. The Word tells us to resist the devil and he will flee. Resist his ways, his tricks, and schemes. Stop letting him use you!
#knowyourstrengthintheLORD #renewyourmind

Submit yourselves, then, to God. Resist the devil, and he will flee from you. James 4:7 NIV

Today, I'm thankful for:

_____
_____
_____
_____
_____
_____
_____
_____

Day 94

Thankful for the purging process. Although it hurts sometimes, it is necessary to rid the impure or undesirable from our bodies and our souls. Go through the cleansing, you'll like the end result!
#wannabemorelikeCHRIST #transforming

If you keep yourself pure, you will be a special utensil for honorable use. Your life will be clean, and you will be ready for the Master to use you for every good work. 2 Timothy 2:21 NLT

Today, I'm thankful for:

_____
_____
_____
_____
_____
_____
_____
_____

Day 95
Thankful for the shedding of the scales from my eyes. The revelation is clear now. God gets the Glory!
#itisbrightouthere

Then Ananias went to the house and entered it. Placing his hands on Saul, he said, "Brother Saul, the Lord--Jesus, who appeared to you on the road as you were coming here--has sent me so that you may see again and be filled with the Holy Spirit." Immediately, something like scales fell from Saul's eyes, and he could see again. He got up and was baptized. **Acts 9:17-18 NIV**

Today, I'm thankful for:

_____
_____
_____
_____
_____
_____
_____
_____

Day 96
Thankful for the hand of God. His way shall always prevail!
#mindrenewing

The heavens declare the glory of God; the skies proclaim the work of his hands. **Psalm 19:1 NIV**

Today, I'm thankful for:

_____
_____
_____
_____
_____
_____
_____
_____

Day 97
Thankful for those who God use to encourage others. Your obedience is not in vain.
#encourageoneanother

***But encourage one another daily, as long as it is called 'Today,' so
that none of you may be hardened by sin's deceitfulness.***
Hebrews 3:13 NIV

Today, I'm thankful for:

_____
_____
_____
_____
_____
_____
_____
_____

Day 98
Thankful for agape love. I still find it amazing how unconditionally He
loves us, even when we don't deserve it.
#gratefulforHislove
#Hislovecoversamultitudeofsins

Hatred stirs up conflict, but love covers over all wrongs.
Proverbs 10:12 NIV

Today, I'm thankful for:

_____
_____
_____
_____
_____
_____
_____

Day 99

Thankful for God's timing. If I received some of the things that I thought I wanted or had to have, I would be sitting somewhere looking crazy by now. His timing is perfect. He knows exactly what we need and when we need it! #Hisloveisperfect #Hisworkisperfect #Heisperfect

The LORD is good to those who wait for him, to the soul who seeks Him. **Lamentations 3:25 ESV**

Today, I'm thankful for:

_____

_____

_____

_____

_____

_____

_____

_____

Day 100

Thankful that I am a friend of God. When no one else will be there, He will.
#friendswithGod

Greater love has no one than this: to lay down one's life for one's friends. **John 15:13 NIV**

Today, I'm thankful for:

_____

_____

_____

_____

_____

_____

_____

_____

Day 101

Thankful for the sudden blessings. No wait, no worry. He loves us that much to do some things suddenly. But know this: He is still *Faithful*, even if we have to wait!
#toknowHimistoloveHim #comequick

And Hezekiah and all the people rejoiced because God had provided for the people, for the thing came about suddenly.
2 Chronicles 29:36 ESV

Today, I'm thankful for:

Day 102

Thankful for God supplying our needs. Yes, He meets every one of our needs. #needsmet

And my God will meet all your needs according to the riches of his glory in Christ Jesus. **Philippians 4:19 NIV**

Today, I'm thankful for:

Day 103
Thankful for His loving-kindness. It is selfless, in spite of me. This love is true Agape love!
#reallove #searchnomore

Whoever does not love does not know God, because God is love.
1 John 4:8 NIV

Today, I'm thankful for:

_____

_____

_____

_____

_____

_____

_____

_____

Day 104
Thankful for the rest I find in His arms. He will hold you close when you need Him to.
#IloveHim #Helovesmemore!

He will cover you with his feathers, and under his wings you will find refuge; his faithfulness will be your shield and rampart.
Psalm 91:4 NIV

Today, I'm thankful for:

_____

_____

_____

_____

_____

_____

_____

_____

Day 105

Thankful for the opportunity to express my Love for the Lord through dance. All things are possible with Him. Use what He has given you to glorify Him.

#giveHimGlory #livingsacrifice

A gift opens the way and ushers the giver into the presence of the great. **Proverbs 18:16 NIV**

Today, I'm thankful for:

_____
_____
_____
_____
_____
_____
_____
_____

Day 106

Thankful for spiritual growth. I'm not what I ought to be but thank God I'm not what I used to be! We should be growing in wisdom, understanding, knowledge, love, patience and all that is good in His eyes.
#stopmakingexcusesforyournegativebehavior
#don'tstaythesame

But grow in the grace and knowledge of our Lord and Savior Jesus Christ. To Him be glory both now and forever! Amen. **2 Peter 3:18 NIV**

Today, I'm thankful for:

_____
_____
_____
_____
_____
_____
_____
_____

Day 107

Thankful for *true* friends! God knows who to send and when to send them. Sometimes the burden is too heavy to bear alone.
#burdenbearers

**Share each other's burdens, and in this way obey the law of Christ.
Galatians 6:2 NLT**

Today, I'm thankful for:

_____

_____

_____

_____

_____

_____

_____

_____

Day 108

Thankful for every mountain that You have brought me over. Lord, I can't walk this walk without You. You change the very existence of my mountains.
#IneedYOULord #mountainshavepeaks&valley

**Every valley shall be filled in, every mountain and hill made low. The crooked roads shall become straight, the rough ways smooth.
Luke 3:5 NIV**

Today, I'm thankful for:

_____

_____

_____

_____

_____

_____

_____

_____

Day 109

Thankful for positive marriages! It's good to see couples investing in the blessings of God!

#yourspouseisablessing #investinyourmarriage

Though one may be overpowered, two can defend themselves. A cord of three strands is not quickly broken. Ecclesiastes 4:12 NIV

Today, I'm thankful for:

_____

_____

_____

_____

_____

_____

_____

_____

Day 110

Thankful for the rays of sunshine. Peace and blessings in the midst of the storm.

#IknowYOUarewithme #YOUaremypeace

Peace I leave with you; my peace I give you. I do not give to you as the world gives. Do not let your hearts be troubled and do not be afraid. John 14:27 NIV

Today, I'm thankful for:

_____

_____

_____

_____

_____

_____

_____

_____

Day 111
Thankful for a great coach – the Holy Spirit. Even when I want to give up, He knows exactly what to say to help me get my head back in the game. #Icandoit

Brothers and sisters, I do not consider myself yet to have taken hold of it. But one thing I do: Forgetting what is behind and straining toward what is ahead, I press on toward the goal to win the prize for which God has called me heavenward in Christ Jesus.
Philippians 3:13-14 NIV

Today, I'm thankful for:

_____
_____
_____
_____
_____
_____
_____
_____

Day 112
Thankful for Jesus rising with *all power* in His hand. All is an inclusive word, so if Jesus has all power, then satan, the enemy, the cologne that brother is wearing, that little red dress, or whatever your vice or temptation, has *no power*.
#stopgivingthempower #dontallowtheweapontoprosper

And Jesus came and spake unto them, saying, All power is given unto me in heaven and in earth. **Matthew 28:18 KJV**

Today, I'm thankful for:

_____
_____
_____
_____
_____
_____
_____

Day 113

Thankful that the old is gone and the new has come. It's a new day, new mercies, new grace, and another chance. Thank you Lord! #livetransformed #makethebestoftoday #enjoyyourpresent

Because of God's tender mercy, the morning light from heaven is about to break upon us, to give light to those who sit in darkness and in the shadow of death, to guide our feet into the path of peace. Luke 1:18-19 NLT

Today, I'm thankful for:

Day 114

Thankful for Jehovah Nissi. Lord you are my banner of Love. #coverus

Let Him lead me to the banquet hall, and let his banner over me be love. Song of Solomon 2:4 NIV

Today, I'm thankful for:

Day 115
Thankful for the power of the Holy Ghost.
#HisSpiritistrue

"But you will receive power when the Holy Spirit has come upon you, and you will be my witnesses in Jerusalem and in all Judea and Samaria, and to the end of the earth." Acts 1:8 ESV

Today, I'm thankful for:

Day 116
Thankful for the opportunity to rejoice in our Heavenly Father. Let us *rejoice* (take delight; make joyful) and be glad! Have a great day in Him.
#whatdoesHedesireofyou

Rejoice in the Lord always. I will say it again: Rejoice! Philippians 4:4 NIV

Today, I'm thankful for:

Day 117

Thankful that you show Yourself mighty in my life. I should have lost my mind by now, but Lord, You have kept me.
#realtalk

Our lives are in his hands, and He keeps our feet from stumbling. You have tested us, O God; you have purified us like silver.
Psalm 66:9-10 NLT

Today, I'm thankful for:

_____

_____

_____

_____

_____

_____

_____

_____

Day 118

Thankful for the pain and suffering that Christ endured for me. He died so that we could live. What are you doing for Him? Let's not be selfish after He was so selfLESS!
#loverofmysoul #justforwhoHeis

And He died for all that those who live should no longer live for themselves but for Him who died for them and was raised again.
2 Corinthians 5:15 NIV

Today, I'm thankful for:

_____

_____

_____

_____

_____

_____

_____

_____

Day 119
Thankful for the truth! Know the truth, it does free you.
#beensetFREE

And ye shall know the truth, and the truth shall make you free.
John 8:32 KJV

Today, I'm thankful for:

_____
_____
_____
_____
_____
_____
_____
_____

Day 120
Thankful for the sun being obedient and shining so brightly these past few
days. Its warmth is comforting.
#thesunisworshipping

If He commands it, the sun won't rise and the stars won't shine.
Job 9:7 NLT

Today, I'm thankful for:

_____
_____
_____
_____
_____
_____
_____
_____

Day 121
Thankful for another day to worship. Ascribe worth and value to our Lord and Savior. He alone is worthy!
#Worshipinspiritandtruth

Great is the LORD! He is most worthy of praise! No one can measure his greatness. Psalm 145:3 NLT

Today, I'm thankful for:

_____

_____

_____

_____

_____

_____

_____

_____

Day 122
Thankful to wake up (that's #1) to birds singing. It is such a beautiful sound of worship!
#myturnnext

I lay down and slept, yet I woke up in safety, for the LORD was watching over me. Psalm 3:5 NLT

Today, I'm thankful for:

_____

_____

_____

_____

_____

_____

_____

_____

Day 123
Thankful for this day that The Lord has made!
#everydayisagreatdaytopraiseHim

**This is the day the LORD has made. We will rejoice and be glad in it.
Psalm 118:24 NLT**

Today, I'm thankful for:

_____
_____
_____
_____
_____
_____
_____
_____

Day 124

Thankful for His love. I don't have to wonder about it. It's real! And guess what? He can and will love you the same. In fact, He has already displayed His Love for you! #Hesacrificedforyou

Love is patient, love is kind. It does not envy, it does not boast, it is not proud. It does not dishonor others, it is not self-seeking, it is not easily angered, it keeps no record of wrongs. Love does not delight in evil but rejoices with the truth. It always protects, always trusts, always hopes, and always perseveres. 1 Corinthians 13:4-7 NIV

Today, I'm thankful for:

_____
_____
_____
_____
_____
_____
_____
_____

Day 125

Thankful for perseverance. It's amazing how God keeps me. There were times I didn't think that I would make it through, but I look up and it's over! You are on the verge of your breakthrough! Hold on! #Heisakeeper #enduranceisthekey

Blessed is the one who perseveres under trial because, having stood the test, that person will receive the crown of life that the Lord has promised to those who love Him. James 1:12 NIV

Today, I'm thankful for:

_____

_____

_____

_____

_____

_____

_____

_____

Day 126

Thankful for God's mercy (not getting what I deserve). #grateful

O give thanks unto the LORD; for He is good: for his mercy endureth forever. Psalm 136:1 KJV

Today, I'm thankful for:

_____

_____

_____

_____

_____

_____

_____

_____

Day 127
Thankful for God's recovery plan. If it has my name on it, I want it!
#gettingmystuffback

David recovered everything the Amalekites had taken, including his two wives. Nothing was missing: young or old, boy or girl, plunder or anything else they had taken. David brought everything back.
1 Samuel 30:18-19 NIV

Today, I'm thankful for:

_____
_____
_____
_____
_____
_____
_____
_____

Day 128
Thankful that my vindication (defense, excuse, justification) is from The Lord! He declared it in His Word.
#HisWordisTrue

He was delivered over to death for our sins and was raised to life for our justification. Therefore, since we have been justified through faith, we have peace with God through our Lord Jesus Christ, through whom we have gained access by faith into this grace in which we now stand. And we boast in the hope of the glory of God.
Romans 4:25-5:2 NIV

Today, I'm thankful for:

_____
_____
_____
_____
_____
_____
_____
_____

Day 129
Thankful that You know me, Lord. You know my heart and my thoughts.
#Youknowmeinsideandout

Search me, God, and know my heart; test me and know my anxious thoughts. See if there is any offensive way in me, and lead me in the way everlasting. **Psalm 139:23-24 NIV**

Today, I'm thankful for:

_____
_____
_____
_____
_____
_____
_____

Day 130
Thankful that I can get excited, even though I don't see the fruit yet!
#Heisworkingitoutforourgood

You shall eat the fruit of the labor of your hands; you shall be blessed, and it shall be well with you. **Psalm 128:2 ESV**

Today, I'm thankful for:

_____
_____
_____
_____
_____
_____
_____

Day 131
Thankful for spiritual maturity! Someone once told me, "Obedience is the highest form of worship."
#notapunk...justobedient
#maturinginHim

But Samuel replied, "What is more pleasing to the LORD: your burnt offerings and sacrifices or your obedience to his voice? Listen! Obedience is better than sacrifice, and submission is better than offering the fat of rams. 1 Samuel 15:22 NLT

Today, I'm thankful for:

_____
_____
_____
_____
_____
_____
_____
_____

Day 132
Thankful for my mother. A mother's love and care are irreplaceable.
#Iloveyoumom

Her children arise and call her blessed. Proverbs 31:28a NIV

Today, I'm thankful for:

_____
_____
_____
_____
_____
_____
_____
_____

Day 133
Thankful for peace and rest in The Lord. He is my refuge!
#Hekeepslookingoutforme

I will say of the LORD, "He is my refuge and my fortress, my God, in whom I trust." Psalm 91:2 NIV

Today, I'm thankful for:

_____

_____

_____

_____

_____

_____

_____

_____

Day 134
Thankful that God is the author and finisher of my Faith because if it *was* man, my story would have probably ended a long time ago.
#mylifeisinHishands

Wherefore seeing we also are compassed about with so great a cloud of witnesses, let us lay aside every weight, and the sin which doth so easily beset us, and let us run with patience the race that is set before us, looking unto Jesus the author and finisher of our faith; who for the joy that was set before Him endured the cross, despising the shame, and is set down at the right hand of the throne of God.
Hebrews 12:1-2 KJV

Today, I'm thankful for:

_____

_____

_____

_____

_____

_____

_____

_____

Day 135
Thankful for the presence of God! He reigns! Blessed be the name of The Lord! #showmeyourglory

Tremble, O earth, at the presence of the Lord, at the presence of the God of Jacob. **Psalm 114:7 NLT**

Today, I'm thankful for:

_____

_____

_____

_____

_____

_____

_____

_____

Day 136
Thankful for like-minded people. People who encourage you when you're going through tough times. People who try their best to live according to the Word of God. People who have a heart's desire to please God in ALL things; not just when they are at a worship center; but in their homes, and on their jobs.
#wearethechurch #livealifepleasingtoGod

Therefore if you have any encouragement from being united with Christ, if any comfort from his love, if any common sharing in the Spirit, if any tenderness and compassion, then make my joy complete by being like-minded, having the same love, being one in spirit and of one mind. **Philippians 2:1-2 NIV**

Today, I'm thankful for:

_____

_____

_____

_____

_____

_____

_____

_____

Day 137
Thankful for ALL blessing which flow from God. I love Him so much and not for material things but just because of who He is.
#Heisawonder #Heisawesome

***For great is the LORD and most worthy of praise; He is to be feared above all gods.* Psalm 96:4 NIV**

Today, I'm thankful for:

_____
_____
_____
_____
_____
_____
_____
_____

Day 138
Thankful for power and authority! Walking in it...in Jesus name! Breaking the chains of bondage.
#Chainsfalling
#powerinthenameofJesus
#brokenforHisGlory

***The heavens belong to the Lord, but He has given the earth to all humanity.* Psalm 115:16 NIV**

Today, I'm thankful for:

_____
_____
_____
_____
_____
_____
_____
_____

Day 139
Thankful that God is helping us to raise respectable and loving children!
Now don't get me wrong, they have their moments. However, they are
truly making us proud!
#gratefulformygifts

**A wise son makes a father glad, But a foolish man despises his
mother. Proverbs 15:20 NASB**

Today, I'm thankful for:

_____
_____
_____
_____
_____
_____
_____
_____

Day 140
Thankful for productive days; handling Kingdom Business!
#takecareofHisbusiness&Hewilltakecareofyours

**Work hard and become a leader; be lazy and become a slave.
Proverbs 12:24 NLT**

Today, I'm thankful for:

_____
_____
_____
_____
_____
_____
_____
_____

Day 141

Thankful for the pruning process. Even though it's painful, it's necessary! In order to be more fruitful, pruning has to take place.
#cutLordcut #iwantmoreofyou

Every branch in me that does not bear fruit He takes away, and every branch that does bear fruit He prunes, that it may bear more fruit.
John 15:2 ESV

Today, I'm thankful for:

_____
_____
_____
_____
_____
_____
_____
_____

Day 142

Thankful for the strength to even get in the Word! He always speaks to me through His Word.
#Heknowstherightthingtosayallthetime
#openTHEBOOK!

Sanctify them by the truth; your word is truth. **John 17:17 NIV**

Today, I'm thankful for:

_____
_____
_____
_____
_____
_____
_____

Day 143
Thankful for another day. Just when you thought you couldn't make it through the sun (SON) rose again!
#Hereallyiswithyou

"The LORD bless you and keep you; the LORD make his face shine on you and be gracious to you; the LORD turn his face toward you and give you peace." **Numbers 6:24:26 NIV**

Today, I'm thankful for:

_____
_____
_____
_____
_____
_____
_____
_____

Day 144
Thankful when God uses me to help make other's dreams come true, and vice versa.
#Heisintheblessingbusiness

"I will make you into a great nation, and I will bless you; I will make your name great, and you will be a blessing. **Genesis 12:2 NIV**

Today, I'm thankful for:

_____
_____
_____
_____
_____
_____
_____
_____

Day 145
Hallelujah! Thankful that His love never fails.
#alwaysontime!

Love never ends. As for prophecies, they will pass away; as for tongues, they will cease; as for knowledge, it will pass away.
1 Corinthians 13:8 ESV

Today, I'm thankful for:

_____

_____

_____

_____

_____

_____

_____

_____

Day 146
Thankful that no matter what type of day I had, God always allows me to sleep peacefully.
#restinHim

In peace I will lie down and sleep, for you alone, LORD, make me dwell in safety. **Psalm 4:8 NIV**

Today, I'm thankful for:

_____

_____

_____

_____

_____

_____

_____

_____

Day 147
Thankful that He (God) never sleeps nor slumbers! He always watches over me.
#HehasHISeyesonyouandI!

He will not let you stumble; the one who watches over you will not slumber. Indeed, He who watches over Israel never slumbers or sleeps. **Psalm 121:3-4 NLT**

Today, I'm thankful for:

_____
_____
_____
_____
_____
_____
_____
_____

Day 148
Thankful for the Holy Ghost and His comfort and guidance.
#inJesusname!

But the Comforter, which is the Holy Ghost, whom the Father will send in my name, He shall teach you all things, and bring all things to your remembrance, whatsoever I have said unto you. **John 14:26 KJV**

Today, I'm thankful for:

_____
_____
_____
_____
_____
_____
_____
_____

Day 149

Thankful that the price was paid! Hallelujah! We don't always get what we deserve.

#wagesofSINisDEATH #Hedidnothavetodoit

For the wages of sin is death, but the gift of God is eternal life in Christ Jesus our Lord. Romans 6:23 NIV

Today, I'm thankful for:

_____

_____

_____

_____

_____

_____

_____

_____

Day 150

Thankful that God's light shines through us.

#GodhasHishandsonus #onlybyHisGrace

Then the righteous will shine like the sun in the kingdom of their Father. Whoever has ears, let them hear. Matthew 13:43 NIV

Today, I'm thankful for:

_____

_____

_____

_____

_____

_____

_____

_____

Day 151
Thankful for your unfailing love and faithfulness.
#HeistheLORD

For the LORD is good. His unfailing love continues forever, and his faithfulness continues to each generation. **Psalm 100:5 NLT**

Today, I'm thankful for:

_____

_____

_____

_____

_____

_____

_____

_____

Day 152
Thankful for the opportunity to serve an EXCELLENT God. Thank you Lord for keeping us!
#Heisexcellentinalltheearth

O LORD our Lord, how excellent is thy name in all the earth! Who hast set thy glory above the heavens. **Psalm 8:1 KJV**

Today, I'm thankful for:

_____

_____

_____

_____

_____

_____

_____

_____

Day 153

Thankful that God doesn't allow us to be tempted beyond what we can bear. Even when we believed that we would never make it through…we looked up and WE made it again.

Breathe in, breathe out; we made it one more day!

#youcanmakeitwithGOD

#Keepmovingandyouwillseetheend

No temptation has overtaken you except what is common to mankind. And God is faithful; He will not let you be tempted beyond what you can bear. But when you are tempted, He will also provide a way out so that you can endure it. **1 Corinthians 10:13 NIV**

Today, I'm thankful for:

_____
_____
_____
_____
_____
_____
_____
_____

Day 154

Thankful for safety in His arms. He is my comforter!

#IcanalwayscountonJesus

Because you are my helper, I sing for joy in the shadow of your wings. **Psalm 63:7 NLT**

Today, I'm thankful for:

_____
_____
_____
_____
_____
_____
_____
_____

Day 155

Thankful that He is always looking out for me!
#myprotector

The LORD himself watches over you! The LORD stands beside you as your protective shade. Psalm 121:5 NLT

Today, I'm thankful for:

_____

_____

_____

_____

_____

_____

_____

_____

Day 156

Thankful that I was called to marriage! Being married can be hard work but it is well worth it when Christ is your center.
#thetwoshallbecomeone

That is why a man leaves his father and mother and is united to his wife, and they become one flesh. Genesis 2:24 NIV

Today, I'm thankful for:

_____

_____

_____

_____

_____

_____

_____

_____

Day 157

Thankful that He keeps me grounded and lifted at the same time!
#Godisgracious
#Hallelujah!

The LORD upholds all who fall and lifts up all who are bowed down.
Psalm 145:14 NIV

Today, I'm thankful for:

Day 158

Thankful that God is still sitting on the throne! No matter the situation, circumstances or challenges you face, He is there.
#searchforHim

Seek the Lord while He may be found; call on Him while He is near.
Isaiah 55:6 NIV

Today, I'm thankful for:

Day 159
Thankful for the opportunity to get away!
#revived
#recharged
#readytohitthegroundrunning

But Jesus Himself would often slip away to the wilderness and pray.
Luke 5:16 NASB

Today, I'm thankful for:

_____

_____

_____

_____

_____

_____

_____

_____

Day 160
Thankful for patience! Although, I don't completely have it down; God is
giving me every opportunity to practice it.
#woooo

My brethren, count it all joy when ye fall into divers temptations;
Knowing this, that the trying of your faith worketh patience.
James 1:2-3 KJV

Today, I'm thankful for:

_____

_____

_____

_____

_____

_____

_____

Day 161

Thankful for the blinders coming off. God sure will reveal things to you when you least expect it.
#scalesstillfalling
#nowIsee

Instantly something like scales fell from Saul's eyes, and he regained his sight. Then he got up and was baptized. Acts 9:18 NLT

Today, I'm thankful for:

_____

_____

_____

_____

_____

_____

_____

_____

Day 162

Thankful for a new days dawning! I saw the sunrise this morning. That means He gave me another chance!
#makingthebestofit

Light is sweet; how pleasant to see a new day dawning. Ecclesiastics 11:7 NLT

Today, I'm thankful for:

_____

_____

_____

_____

_____

_____

_____

_____

Day 163
Thankful that I have a purpose. I was created for something special and so were you!
#bornwithapurpose

For we are his workmanship, created in Christ Jesus for good works, which God prepared beforehand, that we should walk in them.
Ephesians 2:10 NASB

Today, I'm thankful for:

_____
_____
_____
_____
_____
_____
_____
_____

Day 164
Thankful for the snakes that have been biting me. Although it hurt, you have been exposed. I have authority over snakes!
OAN: Lord, please forgive me if I have bitten anyone!
#shakeitoffinthefire
#Goduseshandsthathavebeenbitten

"Behold, I have given you authority to tread on serpents and scorpions, and over all the power of the enemy, and nothing will injure you. Luke 10:19 NASB

Today, I'm thankful for:

_____
_____
_____
_____
_____
_____
_____
_____

Day 165
Thankful for the miracles and blessings that God has for us! Making moves in Jesus name!
#obedienceisbetterthansacrifice

He performs wonders that cannot be fathomed, miracles that cannot be counted. Job 5:9 NIV

Today, I'm thankful for:

_____
_____
_____
_____
_____
_____
_____
_____

Day 166
Thankful that we have freedom to worship the Lord God Almighty!
#nomorebondage
#nomorechains

So if the Son sets you free, you will be free indeed. John 8:36 NIV

Today, I'm thankful for:

_____
_____
_____
_____
_____
_____
_____
_____

Day 167

Thankful for family! Through thick and thin our love will never end! #lovingmyfamily

***Be completely humble and gentle; be patient, bearing with one another in love.* Ephesians 4:2 NIV**

Today, I'm thankful for:

_____

_____

_____

_____

_____

_____

_____

_____

_____

Day 168

Thankful for a faithful God! He is just and righteous in ALL His ways. #faithfulisHe

***The LORD is righteous in all his ways and faithful in all he does.* Psalm 145:17 NIV**

Today, I'm thankful for:

_____

_____

_____

_____

_____

_____

_____

_____

_____

Day 169
Thankful for a personal relationship with our Lord and Savior.
#savedbyHim
#savedforHim

***If you declare with your mouth, "Jesus is Lord," and believe in your heart that God raised Him from the dead, you will be saved.*
Romans 10:9 NIV**

Today, I'm thankful for:

_____

_____

_____

_____

_____

_____

_____

_____

Day 170
Thankful that I don't have to be anxious for anything. I just pray and ask God with Thanksgiving and unexplainable peace will guard my heart and my mind.
#blessed

***Do not be anxious about anything, but in every situation, by prayer and petition, with thanksgiving, present your requests to God.*
Philippians 4:6 NIV**

Today, I'm thankful for:

_____

_____

_____

_____

_____

_____

_____

_____

Day 171
Thankful for celebrations. The way that The Lord blesses my family and friends is life changing. To God be the Glory always!
#ALLtheGLORYbelongstoYOU

Everyone will share the story of your wonderful goodness; they will sing with joy about your righteousness. **Psalm 145:7 NLT**

Today, I'm thankful for:

_____
_____
_____
_____
_____
_____
_____
_____

Day 172
Thankful that God has chosen me to spread His message! He is sovereign and He can use anyone He wants to use. I'm grateful that He chose me.
#thankyouLord
#Yourwaytrumpsall

The heart of man plans his way, but the Lord establishes his steps. **Proverbs 16:9 ESV**

Today, I'm thankful for:

_____
_____
_____
_____
_____
_____
_____
_____

Day 173

Thankful that His Word will never pass away. If He said it, you can stand on it!

#standingonthepromisesofGod

Heaven and earth will pass away, but my words will never pass away. Luke 21:33 NIV

Today, I'm thankful for:

_____

_____

_____

_____

_____

_____

_____

_____

Day 174

Thankful that God has brought me a mighty LONG way. I can't stay the same!

#Godhasthis
#notmybattle

He said: "Listen, King Jehoshaphat and all who live in Judah and Jerusalem! This is what the LORD says to you: 'Do not be afraid or discouraged because of this vast army. For the battle is not yours, but God's. 2 Chronicles 20:15 NIV

Today, I'm thankful for:

_____

_____

_____

_____

_____

_____

_____

_____

Day 175

Thankful that the devil is under our feet. We have to go posse our land.
#hehasnoauthority
#gonow

The God of peace will soon crush Satan under your feet. The grace of our Lord Jesus be with you. Romans 16:20 KJV

Today, I'm thankful for:

_____
_____
_____
_____
_____
_____
_____
_____

Day 176

Thankful for His undying Love! It never ends. I don't ever have to wonder whether or not He loves me. He is consistent in showing me that He does.
#Heissofaithful

Let us hold fast the confession of our hope without wavering, for he who promised is faithful. Hebrew 10:23 ESV

Today, I'm thankful for:

_____
_____
_____
_____
_____
_____
_____
_____

Day 177

Thankful for the ministry of the birds! What a sweet a sound!
#obedienceissweet
#fulfillingpurpose

The birds of the sky nest by the waters; they sing among the branches. **Psalm 104:12 NIV**

Today, I'm thankful for:

_____

_____

_____

_____

_____

_____

_____

_____

Day 178

Thankful that God cares! He will always be there.
#noworries

For all these things the nations of the world eagerly seek; but your Father knows that you need these things. **Luke 12:30 NASB**

Today, I'm thankful for:

_____

_____

_____

_____

_____

_____

_____

_____

Day 179
Thankful that God withholds no good thing from those who walk
uprightly!
#yourbestishere
#walkinrighteousness

**For the LORD God is a sun and shield; the LORD bestows favor and
honor; no good thing does He withhold from those whose walk is
blameless. Psalm 84:11 NIV**

Today, I'm thankful for:

_____

_____

_____

_____

_____

_____

_____

_____

Day 180
Thankful that when I ask God and believe; He does it!
#believeitreceiveit
#YOURwillbedoneLORD
#helpmyunbelief

**Therefore I tell you, whatever you ask for in prayer, believe that you
have received it, and it will be yours. Mark 11:24 NIV**

Today, I'm thankful for:

_____

_____

_____

_____

_____

_____

_____

_____

Day 181
Thankful that my God is a mind regulator. It is my trust and belief in Him that will keep me from being double minded and unstable.
#putonthemindofChrist

A double minded man is unstable in all his ways.
James 1:8 KJV

Today, I'm thankful for:

_____

_____

_____

_____

_____

_____

_____

_____

Day 182
Thankful for my new season. Seasons change, people change but the good thing is our God remains the same!
#sameyesterdaytodayandforevermore

Jesus Christ is the same yesterday and today and forever.
Hebrews 13:8 ESV

Today, I'm thankful for:

_____

_____

_____

_____

_____

_____

_____

_____

Day 183
Thankful that He first loved me! I probably would not have had sense enough to get to know Him on my own.
#HeisaGodofpatience

We love because He first loved us. 1 John 4:19 NIV

Today, I'm thankful for:

_____
_____
_____
_____
_____
_____
_____
_____

Day 184
Thankful for Your Abundance! It keeps coming and coming, and never runs dry.
#supplierofeverything

So shall thy barns be filled with plenty, and thy presses shall burst out with new wine. Proverbs 3:10 KJV

Today, I'm thankful for:

_____
_____
_____
_____
_____
_____
_____
_____

Day 185
Thankful for thoughts that are pure, holy, right and of good rapport amongst all the negativity in the world.
#thinkpositivestaysane
#putitinHishand

Finally, brothers and sisters, whatever is true, whatever is noble, whatever is right, whatever is pure, whatever is lovely, whatever is admirable-if anything is excellent or praiseworthy-think about such things. **Philippians 4:8 NIV**

Today, I'm thankful for:

_____
_____
_____
_____
_____
_____
_____
_____

Day 186
Thankful that my little has the potential to become grand in the Master's hands!
#doit #stepoutonfaith

You give to them, they gather it up; You open Your hand, they are satisfied with good. **Psalm 104:28 NASB**

Today, I'm thankful for:

_____
_____
_____
_____
_____
_____
_____

Day 187
Thankful that God is my source for all things; though He may use others as resources to bless us.
#Heisthesourceandstrengthofmylife

But we know that there is only one God, the Father, who created everything, and we live for Him. And there is only one Lord, Jesus Christ, through whom God made everything and through whom we have been given life. 1 Corinthians 8:6 NLT

Today, I'm thankful for:

_____
_____
_____
_____
_____
_____
_____
_____

Day 188
Thankful that you Lord, hold my world in Your hand.
#IclingtoYou

For I am the Lord your God who takes hold of your right hand and says o you, Do not fear; I will help you. Isaiah 41:13 NIV

Today, I'm thankful for:

_____
_____
_____
_____
_____
_____
_____
_____

Day 189

Thankful that God doesn't break His promises. Wait on the Lord. It will be worth the wait!
#Heisontheway

**Wait for the Lord; be strong and take heart and wait for the Lord.
Psalm 27:14 NIV**

Today, I'm thankful for:

Day 190

Thankful that when I came to the fork in the road, I chose this path. It sometimes gets lonely but I believe in the end, purpose will be fulfilled.
#narrowandlesstraveled

For the gate is narrow and the way is hard that leads to life, and those who find it are few. Matthew 7:14 ESV

Today, I'm thankful for:

Day 191

Thankful for the full armor of God. It protects! I will stand against the devil's schemes.
#gotmyarmoron

Put on the full armor of God, so that you can take your stand against the devil's schemes. Ephesians 6:11 NIV

Today, I'm thankful for:

_____

_____

_____

_____

_____

_____

_____

_____

Day 192

Thankful for second, third, and fourth chances. Lord I am grateful for *all* the opportunities You give me to get it right!
#feelinggrateful

Thanks be to God, who delivers me through Jesus Christ our Lord! So then, I myself in my mind am a slave to God's law, but in my sinful nature a slave to the law sin. Romans 7:25 NIV

Today, I'm thankful for:

_____

_____

_____

_____

_____

_____

_____

_____

Day 193
Thankful that I am blessed to share this journey with a wonderful man of God. Chris Sears, I love you. Happy Birthday!
#July12 #yourRIB #yourgoodthing

The man said, "This is now bone of my bones and flesh of my flesh; she shall be called 'woman,' for she was taken out of man." That is why a man leaves his father and mother and is united to his wife, and they become one flesh. **Genesis 2:23-24 NIV**

Today, I'm thankful for:

_____
_____
_____
_____
_____
_____
_____
_____
_____

Day 194
Thankful for the mindset to train up my gifts in the way that they *should* go. I know that there is a possibility that they may go a different way. But I have faith that when they are old, they will not part from it.
#standingontheWordofGod

Direct your children onto the right path, and when they are older, they will not leave it. **Proverbs 22:6 NLT**

Today, I'm thankful for:

_____
_____
_____
_____
_____
_____
_____
_____

101

Day 195
Thankful for "the Rock!" He (God) is my firm foundation.
#builttolast

The Lord is my rock, my fortress and my deliverer; my God is my rock, in whom I take refuge, my shield and the horn of my salvation, my stronghold. **Psalm 18:2 NIV**

Today, I'm thankful for:

_____
_____
_____
_____
_____
_____
_____
_____

Day 196
Thankful for the encouragement and motivation I receive from others to keep pressing forward!
#lookingahead

Let your eyes look directly forward, and your gaze be straight before you. **Proverbs 4:25 NASB**

Today, I'm thankful for:

_____
_____
_____
_____
_____
_____
_____

Day 197

Thankful that He hides me in the shadow of His wings. Those that try to destroy me shall not prevail.
#safeinHisarms

You are my hiding place; you will protect me from trouble and surround me with songs of deliverance. Psalm 32:7 NIV

Today, I'm thankful for:

_____

_____

_____

_____

_____

_____

_____

_____

Day 198

Thankful that He calls me His own in spite of me!
#Heisworthy

But now thus says the Lord, He who created you, O Jacob, He who formed you, O Israel: "Fear not, for I have redeemed you; I have called you by name, you are mine. Isaiah 43:1-2 ESV

Today, I'm thankful for:

_____

_____

_____

_____

_____

_____

_____

_____

Day 199
Thankful that You are my shield. With You, I am able to withstand fiery darts (test, trials and tribulations) and daggers (gossip, backstabbing and slander) and anything else sent my way.
#Hewillbeyourprotection
#headlifter

But you, Lord, are a shield around me, my glory, the One who lifts my head high. Psalm 3:3 NIV

Today, I'm thankful for:

_____
_____
_____
_____
_____
_____
_____
_____

Day 200
Thankful that the Lord hears my call. Call on His name first!
#trustHim
#Hehasyourback

The Lord is far from the wicked; but He hears the prayer of the righteous. Proverbs 15:29 NIV

Today, I'm thankful for:

_____
_____
_____
_____
_____
_____
_____

Day 201

Thankful that I am an overcomer. When I look back over my life...my God. You are *great* and greatly to be praised!
#itcouldhavebeenme
#GreatGod

**For the LORD is a great God, and a great King above all gods.
Psalm 95:3 ESV**

Today, I'm thankful for:

_____

_____

_____

_____

_____

_____

_____

_____

Day 202

Thankful for the faithful people in my life! There are very few, that I can truly count on but I'm grateful for them.
#accountability

Be devoted to one another in brotherly love; give preference to one another in honor. Romans 12:10 NASB

Today, I'm thankful for:

_____

_____

_____

_____

_____

_____

_____

Day 203

Thankful for dreams becoming reality. God is showing out!
#visionboardiscomingtolife!
#brightfuture

There is surely a future hope for you, and your hope will not be cut off. **Proverbs 23:18 NIV**

Today, I'm thankful for:

_____
_____
_____
_____
_____
_____
_____
_____

Day 204

Thankful that I am chosen in spite of me. Thank you Jesus!
#Hechoseme

You did not choose Me but I chose you, and appointed you that you would go and bear fruit, and that your fruit would remain, so that whatever you ask of the Father in My name He may give you. **John 15:16 NASB**

Today, I'm thankful for:

_____
_____
_____
_____
_____
_____
_____
_____

Day 205
Thankful for prayer and the mindset to believe what I pray!
#talktoGod
#Ibelieve

Let my prayer be set forth before thee as incense, and the lifting up of my hands as the evening sacrifice. Psalm 141:2 KJV

Today, I'm thankful for:

_____

_____

_____

_____

_____

_____

_____

_____

Day 206
Thankful for the conviction of the Holy Ghost! I can't even say or do some of the things that I once had no problem saying or doing.
#guardmymouth
#guidemywalk

I will watch my ways and keep my tongue from sin; I will put a muzzle on my mouth while in the presence of the wicked. Psalm 39:1 NIV

Today, I'm thankful for:

_____

_____

_____

_____

_____

_____

_____

_____

Day 207
Thankful for the opportunity to be an extension of the hand of God.
Thank you Lord for using me!
#cheerfulgiver
#muchinHishands

Each one must give as he has decided in his heart, not reluctantly or under compulsion, for God loves a cheerful giver.
2 Corinthians 9:7 ESV

Today, I'm thankful for:

_____

_____

_____

_____

_____

_____

_____

_____

Day 208
Thankful that I don't have to be ashamed of my past anymore. He has washed me with His blood.
#forgiven
#purified

If we confess our sins, He is faithful and just and will forgive us our sins and purify us from all unrighteousness. **1 John 1:9 NIV**

Today, I'm thankful for:

_____

_____

_____

_____

_____

_____

_____

_____

Day 209

Thankful that God allows me to make a positive impact in the lives of others. My heart's desire is to help.
#GlorytoGodinthehighest
#thegiftofhelps

Give, and it will be given to you. A good measure, pressed down, shaken together and running over, will be poured into your lap. For with the measure you use, it will be measured to you. Luke 6:38 NIV

Today, I'm thankful for:

_____

_____

_____

_____

_____

_____

_____

_____

Day 210

Thankful for the knowledge to glean wisdom. Knowledge is power!
#gainingwisdom
#littlebylittle

Teach me good discernment and knowledge, for I believe in Your commandments. Psalm 119:66 NASB

Today, I'm thankful for:

_____

_____

_____

_____

_____

_____

_____

_____

Day 211
Thankful that He meets me when I need Him most. He hides me. In Your presence is where I want to be.
#IwilldoanythingforHisGlory
#Hispresence

In the cover of your presence you hide them from the plots of men; you store them in your shelter from the strife of tongues.
Psalm 31:20 ESV

Today, I'm thankful for:

_____
_____
_____
_____
_____
_____
_____
_____

Day 212
Thankful that I became a different statistic. But God! His plans are great.
#HisplanHispurpose
#orderedsteps

The steps of a man are established by the LORD, And He delights in his way. Psalm 37:23 NASB

Today, I'm thankful for:

_____
_____
_____
_____
_____
_____
_____
_____

Day 213

Thankful for the process of thought. If I didn't think before I reacted, I would be in a world of trouble but so would some other people.
#everyonedoesn'thavetoknowwhatyoufeel

A gentle answer turns away wrath, but a harsh word stirs up anger.
Proverbs 15:1 NIV

Today, I'm thankful for:

Day 214

Thankful for the perfect example that He sent in His son. We should strive daily to do as Jesus would do.
#intheworldnotoftheworld

Follow God's example, therefore, as dearly loved children and walk in the way of love, just as Christ loved us and gave himself up for us as a fragrant offering and sacrifice to God. **Ephesians 5:1-2 NIV**

Today, I'm thankful for:

Day 215
Thankful for the Scriptures. If we are diligent students, we can learn what
to do and what *not* to do.
#thepastshouldteachyou
#itispartofyourjourney

**For everything that was written in the past was written to teach us, so
that through the endurance taught in the Scriptures and the
encouragement they provide we might have hope. Romans 15:4 NIV**

Today, I'm thankful for:

_____
_____
_____
_____
_____
_____
_____
_____

Day 216
Thankful that God has allowed me to accomplish a major goal of mine!
#moretocome
#ItispossiblewithHim

**Take delight in the Lord, and He will give you the desires of your
heart. Psalm 37:4 NIV**

Today, I'm thankful for:

_____
_____
_____
_____
_____
_____
_____
_____

Day 217
Thankful that all things are working together for my good. Hallelujah! Do you love Him? Have you been called according to His purpose? Then it's going to work out for you as well.
#YesIdoloveHim

And we know that in all things God works for the good of those who love Him, who have called according to his purpose.
Romans 8:28 NIV

Today, I'm thankful for:

_____
_____
_____
_____
_____
_____
_____
_____

Day 218
Thankful that the Lord causes my enemies to flee!
#byesatan

The Lord will grant that the enemies who rise up against you will be defeated before you. They will come at you from one direction but flee from you in seven. **Deuteronomy 28:7 NIV**

Today, I'm thankful for:

_____
_____
_____
_____
_____
_____
_____
_____

Day 219
Thankful for the godly women and men that God has allowed to cross my path.
#ironsharpensiron

As iron sharpens iron, so one person sharpens another.
Proverbs 27:17 NIV

Today, I'm thankful for:

_____
_____
_____
_____
_____
_____
_____
_____

Day 220
Thankful that God comes to see about His children when we cry out to Him!
#Heisthere
#omnipresent

Where can I go from your Spirit? Where can I flee from your presence? If I go up to the heavens, you are there; if I make my bed in the depths, you are there. If I rise on the wings of the dawn, if I settle on the far side of the sea, even there your hand will guide me, your right hand will hold me fast. Psalm 139:7-10 NIV

Today, I'm thankful for:

_____
_____
_____
_____
_____
_____
_____
_____

Day 221

Thankful for God clearing the path. Whether on land or sea, He is more than capable to do it.

#thankyouLord #waymaker

I am the Lord, who opened a way through the waters, making a dry path through the sea. I called forth the mighty army of Egypt with all its chariots and horses. I drew them beneath the waves, and they drowned, their lives snuffed out like a smoldering candlewick. "But forget all that—it is nothing compared to what I am going to do. For I am about to do something new. See, I have already begun! Do you not see it? I will make a pathway through the wilderness. I will create rivers in the dry wasteland. **Isaiah 43:16-19 NLT**

Today, I'm thankful for:

_____

_____

_____

_____

_____

_____

_____

_____

Day 222

Thankful that when God says yes, it doesn't matter what anyone else says.

#Hisyesmeanssomuch

For no matter how many promises God has made, they are "Yes" in Christ. And so through Him the "Amen" is spoken by us to the glory of God. **2 Corinthians 1:20 NIV**

Today, I'm thankful for:

_____

_____

_____

_____

_____

_____

_____

_____

Day 223

Thankful for the spirit of conviction. It causes me to think about the possible consequences and make an informed choice. Sometimes it's not an easy path to follow however, with God, all things are possible!
#thinkaboutitfirst

Jesus Looked at them and said, "With man this is impossible, but with God all things are possible." Matthew 19:26 NIV

Today, I'm thankful for:

_____

_____

_____

_____

_____

_____

_____

_____

Day 224

Thankful for visions and dreams! The best is here. What are you going to do with it?
#whatareyouwaitingfor

Indeed, the Sovereign Lord never does anything until He reveals his plans to his servants the prophets. Amos 3:7 NLT

Today, I'm thankful for:

_____

_____

_____

_____

_____

_____

_____

_____

Day 225
Thankful that the Lord reigns in my life!
#YouReign

The Lord reigns forever, your God, O Zion, for all generations. Praise the Lord. Psalm 146:10 NIV

Today, I'm thankful for:

_____
_____
_____
_____
_____
_____
_____
_____

Day 226
Thankful for the times when the Holy Ghost comes in like a rushing stream.
#sweepthroughthisplace

So they shall fear the name of the Lord from the west, and his glory from the rising of the sun; for He will come like a rushing stream, which the wind of the Lord drives. Isaiah 59:19 ESV

Today, I'm thankful for:

_____
_____
_____
_____
_____
_____
_____
_____

Day 227
Thankful that when we humble ourselves, He exalts us!
#ohtoberaisedupbytheLord

Humble *yourselves before the Lord, and He will lift you up.*
James 4:10 NIV

Today, I'm thankful for:

_____
_____
_____
_____
_____
_____
_____
_____

Day 228
Thankful that grace is my portion through humility.
#Hegivesgracetothehumble

"But by the grace of God I am what I am, and his grace toward me
was not in vain. On the contrary, I worked harder than any of them,
though it was not I, but the grace of God that is with me."
1 Corinthians 15:10 ESV

Today, I'm thankful for:

_____
_____
_____
_____
_____
_____
_____
_____

Day 229
Thankful that praise brings forth breakthrough. Need a breakthrough? I dare you praise Him!
#commandyoursoultoblessTheLord

Praise the Lord, my soul, and forget not all his benefits—who forgives all your sins and heals all your diseases, who redeems your life from the pit and crowns you with love and compassion, who satisfies your desires with good things so that your youth is renewed like the eagle's. Psalm 103:2-5 NIV

Today, I'm thankful for:

_____
_____
_____
_____
_____
_____
_____
_____

Day 230
Thankful for another day to serve my family. Do EVERYTHING as unto the Lord.
#feelingblessed
#withyourwholeheart

Whatever you do, work at it with all your heart, as working for the Lord, not for human masters. Colossians 3:23 NIV

Today, I'm thankful for:

_____
_____
_____
_____
_____
_____
_____

Day 231
Thankful that I serve a God that has my best interest at heart! He always knows what's best for me.
#looktothehills
#yourhelpcomesfromtheLord

I lift up my eyes to the mountains—where does my help come from? My help come from the Lord, the Maker of heaven and earth. **Psalm 121:2-3 NIV**

Today, I'm thankful for:

_____
_____
_____
_____
_____
_____
_____
_____

Day 232
Thankful for Him increasing my Faith. Sometimes the challenges appear difficult. However, when I keep walking and talking with Him, I look up and it's done!
#keepyourmindstayedonHim
#dontshiftyourfocus

For we live by faith, not by sight. **2 Corinthians 5:7 NIV**

Today, I'm thankful for:

_____
_____
_____
_____
_____
_____
_____

Day 233

Thankful that God is not a liar! If He said it, He will do it.
#faithactivated

God is not human, that He should lie, not a human being, that He should change his mind. Does He speak and then not act? Does He promise and not fulfill? **Numbers 23:19 NIV**

Today, I'm thankful for:

_____

_____

_____

_____

_____

_____

_____

Day 234

Thankful for new creativity! You keep on blessing me.
#wowHedidthat!

Do you see a man skillful in his work? He will stand before kings; he will not stand before obscure men. **Proverbs 22:29 ESV**

Today, I'm thankful for:

_____

_____

_____

_____

_____

_____

_____

Day 235
Thankful for His keeping power! He is truly a keeper.
#believethat

Keep me, O LORD, from the hands of the wicked; preserve me from the violent man; who have purposed to overthrow my goings.
Psalm 140:4 KJV

Today, I'm thankful for:

_____
_____
_____
_____
_____
_____
_____
_____

Day 236
Thankful that we can pay our bills. Debts being paid!
#Debtfreedomcomingsoon

The rich rule over the poor, and the borrower is slave to the lender.
Proverbs 22:7 NIV

Today, I'm thankful for:

_____
_____
_____
_____
_____
_____
_____
_____

Day 237
Thankful for the power of prayer! It truly does work. Even if it doesn't change your situation, it can change your perspective.
#praytheWord
#prayHisWill

I consider that our present sufferings are not worth comparing with the glory that will be revealed in us. **Romans 8:18 NIV**

Today, I'm thankful for:

_____
_____
_____
_____
_____
_____
_____
_____

Day 238
Thankful that He is the Good Shepherd. He knows more about me than I know about myself.
#timeout
#Heknowsme

"I am the good shepherd. The good shepherd lays down his life for the sheep." **John 10:11 NIV**

Today, I'm thankful for:

_____
_____
_____
_____
_____
_____
_____
_____

Day 239
Thankful for these quiet moments. I need to do this more often - shut out all distractions.
#sittingontheporch
#readingabook

Be still before the Lord and wait patiently for Him; do not fret when people succeed in their ways, when they carry out their wicked schemes. Psalm 37:7 NIV

Today, I'm thankful for:

_____
_____
_____
_____
_____
_____
_____
_____
_____

Day 240
Thankful that we are *not* defeated! We have the *victory* in Jesus!
#thedevilisaliar
#donotbelievehishype

But thanks be to God! He gives us the victory through our Lord Jesus Christ. 1 Corinthians 15:57 NIV

Today, I'm thankful for:

_____
_____
_____
_____
_____
_____
_____
_____
_____

Day 241
Thankful for being able to see God's glory in His vast creation.
#Hetrulyisawesome

For the earth will be filled with the knowledge of the glory of the Lord as the waters cover the sea. Habakkuk 2:14 NIV

Today, I'm thankful for:

_____
_____
_____
_____
_____
_____
_____
_____

Day 242
Thankful for harvest time! You have sown; now the time has come for you to reap.
#Donotfaint
#itishere!
#hallelujah

Let us not become weary in doing good, for at the proper time we will reap a harvest if we do not give up. Galatians 6:9 NIV

Today, I'm thankful for:

_____
_____
_____
_____
_____
_____
_____
_____

Day 243
Thankful for an enlarged territory to do His will!
#blessed
#worktobedone

Jabez cried out to the God of Israel, "Oh, that you would bless me and enlarge my territory! Let your hand be with me, and keep me from harm so that I will be free from pain." And God granted his request. **1 Chronicles 4:10 NIV**

Today, I'm thankful for:

_____
_____
_____
_____
_____
_____
_____
_____

Day 244
Thankful for the endless possibilities that come with my relationship with Christ!
#itallbelongstoGod
#theblessingisonyou

O Sovereign Lord! You made the heavens and earth by your strong hand and powerful arm. Nothing is too hard for you! **Jeremiah 32:17 NLT**

Today, I'm thankful for:

_____
_____
_____
_____
_____
_____
_____
_____

Day 245
Thankful for *all* the doors He has opened for me!
#Hekeepsonlookingoutforme
#wecannotdenyHim

I know your deeds. See, I have placed before you an open door that no one can shut. I know that you have little strength, yet you have kept my word and have not denied my name. **Revelation 3:8 NIV**

Today, I'm thankful for:

_____
_____
_____
_____
_____
_____
_____
_____

Day 246
Thankful for the "ram in the bush." God's timing is always perfect! Trust Him.
#ontimeeverytime

Then Abraham looked up and saw a ram caught by its horns in a thicket. So he took the ram and sacrificed it as a burnt offering in place of his son. **Genesis 22:13 NLT**

Today, I'm thankful for:

_____
_____
_____
_____
_____
_____
_____
_____

Day 247
Thankful for new heights and new levels! Moving on up a little higher in Jesus name.
#Heliftsmeup
#cannotfightwithFAVOR

May the favor of the Lord our God rest on us; establish the work of our hands for us-- yes, establish the work of our hands.
Psalm 90:17 NIV

Today, I'm thankful for:

_____

_____

_____

_____

_____

_____

_____

_____

Day 248
Thankful for the honest people in my life. Honesty truly does pay.
#youreapwhatyousow
#honestyisthebestpolicy

All you need to say is simply "Yes" or "No"; anything beyond this comes from the evil one. Matthew 5:37 NIV

Today, I'm thankful for:

_____

_____

_____

_____

_____

_____

_____

_____

Day 249

Thankful that *nothing* can separate us from the love of God. He loves us just that *much*!

#embracedbyChrist

And I am convinced that nothing can ever separate us from God's love. Neither death nor life, neither angels nor demons, neither our fears for today nor our worries about tomorrow—not even the powers of hell can separate us from God's love. Romans 8:38 NLT

Today, I'm thankful for:

_____
_____
_____
_____
_____
_____
_____
_____

Day 250

Thankful that I can't lose with Christ on my side! No matter what it looks like, in the end I always win.

#winning

For everyone who has been born of God overcomes the world. And this is the victory that has overcome the world—our faith. 1 John 5:4 ESV

Today, I'm thankful for:

_____
_____
_____
_____
_____
_____
_____
_____

Day 251

Thankful for God's generosity! If I lack anything, all I have to do is ask.
#Hiskindnessisvast #Openyourmouth

***You want what you don't have, so you scheme and kill to get it. You are jealous of what others have, but you can't get it, so you fight and wage war to take it away from them. Yet you don't have what you want because you don't ask God for it.* James 4:2 NLT**

Today, I'm thankful for:

_____

_____

_____

_____

_____

_____

_____

_____

Day 252

Thankful that I don't have to worry. Even though I sometimes choose to, He is still working on me. I can stand on His Word. Anybody else have a "from now on spirit?"
#hesuppliesALLmyneed #prayingfromnowon
#believingfromnowon #trustingfromnowon
#noworriesFORREAL

***Therefore do not worry about tomorrow, for tomorrow will worry about itself. Each day has enough trouble of its own.*
Matthew 6:34 NIV**

Today, I'm thankful for:

_____

_____

_____

_____

_____

_____

_____

_____

Day 253

Thankful for stability of the mind. No longer doubting my God.

#cannotservetwomasters

#NOtimetobedoubleminded

#Work in progress

But when you ask, you must believe and not doubt, because the one who doubts is like a wave of the sea, blown and tossed by the wind. That person should not expect to receive anything from the Lord. Such a person is double-minded and unstable in all they do. **James 1:6-8 NIV**

Today, I'm thankful for:

_____

_____

_____

_____

_____

_____

_____

_____

Day 254

Thankful that all my senses are in working order this morning.

#eyestosee

#earstohear

But blessed are your eyes because they see, and your ears because they hear. **Matthew 13:16 NIV**

Today, I'm thankful for:

_____

_____

_____

_____

_____

_____

_____

_____

Day 255
Thankful for the seeds God has sown through me! What a blessing to be used in the name of the Lord.
#notfainting
#itsHarvesttime

He who supplies seed to the sower and bread for food will supply and multiply your seed for sowing and increase the harvest of your righteousness. **2 Corinthians 9:10 ESV**

Today, I'm thankful for:

_____

_____

_____

_____

_____

_____

_____

_____

Day 256
Thankful for every blessing, especially the small ones, for they are a constant reminder of how much He truly loves me!
#ohhowHelovesme
#THANKSforeverything

Be thankful in all circumstances, for this is God's will for you who belong to Christ Jesus. **1 Thessalonians 5:18 NLT**

Today, I'm thankful for:

_____

_____

_____

_____

_____

_____

_____

_____

Day 257
Thankful for a cup running over! He keeps on blessing me.
#itsspillingout

You prepare a table before me in the presence of my enemies. You anoint my head with oil; my cup overflows. **Psalm 23:5 NIV**

Today, I'm thankful for:

_____
_____
_____
_____
_____
_____
_____
_____
_____

Day 258
Thankful that through Christ I can do *anything*!
#yesitispossible
#livingwitness

I can do all things through Christ which strengthened me. **Philippians 4:13 KJV**

Today, I'm thankful for:

_____
_____
_____
_____
_____
_____
_____
_____
_____

Day 259
Thankful that when I adhere to the prompting of the Holy Spirit, I stay out
of so much trouble!
#dieflesh

So I say, walk by the Spirit, and you will not gratify the desires of the
flesh. For the flesh desires what is contrary to the Spirit, and the
Spirit what is contrary to the flesh. They are in conflict with each
other, so that you are not to do whatever you want.
Galatians 5:16-17 NIV

Today, I'm thankful for:

_____

_____

_____

_____

_____

_____

_____

_____

Day 260
Thankful for the fear of The Lord; for it is the beginning of wisdom and
knowledge.
#reverenceHim

Fear of the Lord is the foundation of wisdom. Knowledge of the Holy
One results in good judgment. **Proverbs 9:10 NLT**

Today, I'm thankful for:

_____

_____

_____

_____

_____

_____

_____

_____

Day 261
Faith + Works = Blessings in the best way - His way!
#workthatFaith

You see that a person is justified by works and not by faith alone.
James 2:24 ESV

Today, I'm thankful for:

Day 262
Thankful that even in the midst of Him disciplining us, He shows us mercy.
#TheStory
#becauseHelovesus

For thou, Lord art good, and ready to forgive; and plenteous in mercy
unto all them that call upon thee. Psalm 86:5 KJV

Today, I'm thankful for:

Day 263
Thankful that we have the power to overcome sin by His word.
#dontletitovertakeyou
#exerciseyourpower
#lookforthewayofexcape

I have hidden your word in my heart that I might not sin against you.
Psalm 119:11 NIV

Today, I'm thankful for:

_____
_____
_____
_____
_____
_____
_____
_____

Day 264
Thankful that when I do what The Lord commands, blessings follow.
#theflow
#blessed

If you fully obey the Lord your God and carefully follow all his commands I give you today, the Lord your God will set you high above all the nations on earth. **Deuteronomy 28:1 NIV**

Today, I'm thankful for:

_____
_____
_____
_____
_____
_____
_____
_____

Day 265
Thankful that when God promises the impossible, He can, and will deliver!
#walkinginFaith

Jesus replied, "What is impossible with man is possible with God."
Luke 18:27 NIV

Today, I'm thankful for:

_____

_____

_____

_____

_____

_____

_____

_____

Day 266
Thankful that You Lord, see the depths of our hearts and you reward us
accordingly.
#YouareanamazingGod
#incomparable

***I the Lord search the heart and examine the mind, to reward each
person according to their conduct, according to what their deeds
deserve.* Jeremiah 17:10 NIV**

Today, I'm thankful for:

_____

_____

_____

_____

_____

_____

_____

_____

Day 267
Thankful for the journey. This walk has not been easy but the testimony is sure to bless the lives of others. Don't be ashamed share with others as the Lord leads you.
#defeattheenemy…shareyourtestimony
#someoneslifedependsonit

And they overcame him by the blood of the Lamb, and by the word of their testimony; and they loved not their lives unto the death.
Revelation 12:11 KJV

Today, I'm thankful for:

_____
_____
_____
_____
_____
_____
_____
_____

Day 268
Thankful that He is there to keep me from stumbling. He makes me look good for His name sake.
#nopeNOTperfect

To him who is able to keep you from stumbling and to present you before his glorious presence without fault and with great joy.
Jude 1:24 NIV

Today, I'm thankful for:

_____
_____
_____
_____
_____
_____
_____

Day 269
Thankful that I serve a perfect God, even when things in my life don't seem so perfect.
#yesthatisHim

"As for God, his way is perfect: The LORD's word is flawless; He shields all who take refuge in Him." 2 Samuel 22:31 NIV

Today, I'm thankful for:

_____

_____

_____

_____

_____

_____

_____

_____

Day 270
Thankful for the call to order. God is *not* the author of confusion!
#inline
#peaceNOTchaos

For God is not the author of confusion, but of peace, as in all churches of the saints. 1 Corinthians 14:33 KJV

Today, I'm thankful for:

_____

_____

_____

_____

_____

_____

_____

_____

Day 271
Thankful that when I'm feeling "woe is me," God shows me what it could
have been. He gives me the grace to move on!
#feelingappreciative
#itcouldhavebeenmeButGod

**So let us come boldly to the throne of our gracious God. There we
will receive his mercy, and we will find grace to help us when we
need it most.** Hebrews 4:16 NLT

Today, I'm thankful for:

_____

_____

_____

_____

_____

_____

_____

_____

Day 272
Thankful for the subtle reminders that God allows me to experience. They
help me to try that much harder to stay on His path for me.
#walkinobedience

**Stay on the path that the LORD your God has commanded you to
follow. Then you will live long and prosperous lives in the land you
are about to enter and occupy.** Deuteronomy 5:33 NLT

Today, I'm thankful for:

_____

_____

_____

_____

_____

_____

_____

Day 273
Thankful for my relationship with the Lord, He keeps me right. I can't do it by myself.
#purifymyheartandcleansemyhands

Examine me, O Lord, and try me; Test my mind and my heart.
Psalm 26:2 NSAB

Today, I'm thankful for:

_____
_____
_____
_____
_____
_____
_____
_____

Day 274
Thankful that God knows every intricate detail about me and yet He still loves me. He knew me before I was even formed.
#weareconnected
#IloveHim

"Before I formed you in the womb I knew you, before you were born I set you apart; I appointed you as a prophet to the nations."
Jeremiah 1:5 NIV

Today, I'm thankful for:

_____
_____
_____
_____
_____
_____
_____

Day 275
Thankful for the mighty hand of God! It exalts, it humbles, it saves, and it has all power.
#pleasekeepyourHandsonme

Humble yourselves, therefore, under God's mighty hand, that He may lift you up in due time. 1 Peter 5:6 NIV

Today, I'm thankful for:

_____
_____
_____
_____
_____
_____
_____
_____

Day 276
Thankful for His overwhelming *love*! You won't find anything like it.
#LoveofGod #itrunsdeep

But because of His great love for us, God, who is rich in mercy, made us alive with Christ even when we were dead in transgressions—it is by grace you have been saved. Ephesians 2:4-5 NIV

Today, I'm thankful for:

_____
_____
_____
_____
_____
_____
_____
_____

Day 277

Thankful that He intimately knows me. It is my desire to know Him more intimately.

#knowsthenumberofhairsonmyhead

And the very hairs on your head are all numbered.
Matthew 10:30 NLT

Today, I'm thankful for:

Day 278

Thankful that you hear my cry for mercy and you help me.

#hearmeOLord

Out of the depths I cry to you, Lord; Lord, hear my voice. Let your ears be attentive to my cry for mercy. Psalm 130:1-2 NIV

Today, I'm thankful for:

Day 279
Thankful that I serve a *great* and *powerful* God.
#HeistheLord
#idonthavetowonder

Your ways, God are holy. What god is as great as our God?
Psalm 77:13 NIV

Today, I'm thankful for:

_____
_____
_____
_____
_____
_____
_____
_____

Day 280
Thankful that there is *no* condemnation in Christ Jesus!
#thebloodstillworks
#forgiven

Therefore, there is now no condemnation for those who are in Christ
Jesus, because through Christ Jesus the law of the Spirit who gives
life has set you free from the law of sin and death.
Romans 8:1-2 NIV

Today, I'm thankful for:

_____
_____
_____
_____
_____
_____
_____
_____

Day 281
Thankful that He keeps my foot from getting trapped. I am confident in Him.
#Hehasyourbackwhenothersdonot

For the LORD will be your confidence and will keep your foot from being caught. Proverbs 3:26 NASB

Today, I'm thankful for:

_____

_____
_____
_____
_____
_____
_____
_____
_____

Day 282
Thankful that You, Lord, are my strength and portion. My eternal love!
#MyheartisforHim

My flesh and my heart may fail, but God is the strength of my heart and my portion forever. Psalm 73:26 NIV

Today, I'm thankful for:

_____

_____
_____
_____
_____
_____
_____
_____

Day 283

Thankful that God is turning my situation around! There is a purpose for what we go through.
#HehasturnaroundPower

I cry out to God Most High, to God who will fulfill his purpose for me. **Psalm 57:2 NLT**

Today, I'm thankful for:

_____

_____

_____

_____

_____

_____

_____

_____

Day 284

Thankful that my life is in His hands! There is no better place to be.
#itiswell

My times are in your hands; deliver me from the hands of my enemies from those who pursue me. **Psalm 31:15 NIV**

Today, I'm thankful for:

_____

_____

_____

_____

_____

_____

_____

_____

Day 285
Thankful that even when it doesn't work out the way that I think it should,
I can still say I trust Him.
#trustHim
#Heknowsbest

Every word of God is pure: He is a shield unto them that put their trust in Him. Proverbs 30:5 KJV

Today, I'm thankful for:

_____

_____

_____

_____

_____

_____

_____

_____

Day 286
Thankful for a heart to please God.
#SaytheWordandIwillobey

So whether we are at home or away, we make it our aim to please Him. 2 Corinthians 5:9 ESV

Today, I'm thankful for:

_____

_____

_____

_____

_____

_____

_____

_____

Day 287
Thankful for the Faith to follow. Even when I can't see my way, I'll trust You.
#keepmoving
#evidenceofthingsNOTseen

Commit thy way unto the Lord; trust also in Him; and He shall bring it to pass. **Psalm 37:5 KJV**

Today, I'm thankful for:

_____
_____
_____
_____
_____
_____
_____
_____

Day 288
Thankful that the mind of Christ is available to us. Use what you have been given.
#letthismindbeinyou

"For who has understood the mind of the Lord so as to instruct Him?" But we have the mind of Christ. **1 Corinthians 2:16 ESV**

Today, I'm thankful for:

_____
_____
_____
_____
_____
_____
_____
_____

Day 289
Thankful that even when others don't keep their promises, His promises
never fail.
#promisekeeper
#dependonHim

For no word from God will ever fail. Luke 1:37 NIV

Today, I'm thankful for:

_____
_____
_____
_____
_____
_____
_____
_____

Day 290
Thankful that I am *more* than a conqueror in Christ Jesus!
#thebenefitstobeinginChrist

**Nay, in all these things we are more than conquerors through Him
that loved us.** Romans 8:37 KJV

Today, I'm thankful for:

_____
_____
_____
_____
_____
_____
_____
_____

Day 291
Thankful that The Lord will fight for me while I keep silent.
#thebattleisHis

The Lord Himself will fight for you. Just stay calm.
Exodus 14:14 NLT

Today, I'm thankful for:

_____
_____
_____
_____
_____
_____
_____
_____

Day 292
Thankful for *freedom* in Christ. I will not live life bound!
#chainsbroken
#weightslifted

It is for freedom that Christ has set us free. Stand firm, then, and do
not let yourselves be burdened again by a yoke of slavery.
Galatians 5:1 NIV

Today, I'm thankful for:

_____
_____
_____
_____
_____
_____
_____
_____

Day 293
Thankful that I serve a big "G" - God! Small "g" – gods - have *no* power!
#powerinHisname
#allPowerinHishand

By his power God raised the Lord from the dead, and He will raise us also. 1 Corinthians 6:14 NIV

Today, I'm thankful for:

_____
_____
_____
_____
_____
_____
_____
_____

Day 294
Thankful for boldness in Christ! Tap in and be a powerful witness for the Kingdom of God!
#beboldinHim
#Heisgreatness

**I will speak to kings about your laws, and I will not be ashamed.
Psalm 119:46 NLT**

Today, I'm thankful for:

_____
_____
_____
_____
_____
_____
_____

Day 295
Thankful for the extraordinary *power* in Jesus' name! At the name of Jesus, the impossible is made possible.
#sayHisname
#JESUS

It is He who made the earth by his power, who established the world by his wisdom, and by his understanding stretched out the heavens. Jeremiah 10:12 ESV

Today, I'm thankful for:

_____
_____
_____
_____
_____
_____
_____
_____

Day 296
Thankful for blessings both coming and going. He has us covered.
#cityandfieldblessings
#blessedbythemaster

Blessed shall you be when you come in and blessed shall you be when you got out. Deuteronomy 28:6 ESV

Today, I'm thankful for:

_____
_____
_____
_____
_____
_____
_____
_____

Day 297
Thankful for the abundance of *love* He continues to shower me with.
#Heisjealousforme
#HisLoveispatient

This how God showed His love among us: He sent His one and only Son into the world that we might live through Him. This is love: not that we loved God, but that He loved us and sent His Son as an atoning sacrifice for our sins. 1 John 4:9-10 NIV

Today, I'm thankful for:

_____

_____

_____

_____

_____

_____

_____

_____

Day 298
Thankful that seasons change. It won't always be like this.
#keeptheFaith

For everything there is a season, a time for every activity under heaven. Ecclesiastes 3:1 NLT

Today, I'm thankful for:

_____

_____

_____

_____

_____

_____

_____

_____

Day 299

Thankful for a mountain moving God! Sometimes, when you can't seem to get over it or know how to get around it, the Savior will come by and just move it out the way.

#moveouttheway

The mountains melt like wax before the Lord, before the Lord of all the earth. Psalm 97:5 NIV

Today, I'm thankful for:

_____

_____

_____

_____

_____

_____

_____

_____

Day 300

Thankful that God is for me, so it doesn't matter who is against me.

#IamonHisteamHeisonmyteam #Hehasmyback

For those God foreknew He also predestined to be conformed to the image of His Son, that He might be the firstborn among many brothers and sisters. And those He predestined, He also called; those He called, He also justified; those He justified, He also glorified. What, then, shall we say in response to these things? If God is for us, who can be against us? Romans 8:29-31 NIV

Today, I'm thankful for:

_____

_____

_____

_____

_____

_____

_____

_____

Day 301

Thankful that even when it doesn't look like it, He is working it out for our good!

#lovingHim

#calledaccordingtoHispurpose

For God is working in you, giving you the desire and the power to do what pleases Him. Philippians 2:13 NLT

Today, I'm thankful for:

_____

_____

_____

_____

_____

_____

_____

_____

Day 302

Thankful that He called me out of darkness. His light shines through me.

#chosenpeople

#IbelongtoGod

But you are a chosen race, a royal priesthood, a holy nation, a people for His own possession, that you may proclaim the excellences of Him who called you of darkness into His marvelous light. 1 Peter 2:9 ESV

Today, I'm thankful for:

_____

_____

_____

_____

_____

_____

_____

_____

Day 303

Thankful for the desire to endure. There have been so many times that I have wanted to give up in many areas of life but God always sends the encouragement to *press on*.

#keeponmoving

Rejoice in hope, be patient in tribulation, be constant in prayer.
Romans 12:12 ESV

Today, I'm thankful for:

_____

_____

_____

_____

_____

_____

_____

_____

Day 304

Thankful that even when it looks like things are out of control, God is still in control.

#trustHim

Our God is in heaven; He does whatever pleases Him.
Psalm 115:3 NIV

Today, I'm thankful for:

_____

_____

_____

_____

_____

_____

_____

Day 305
Thankful for a contrite heart; a heart filled with a sense of guilt and the desire for atonement. I have been redeemed!
#broken #Hecanfixit

***The sacrifices of God are a broken spirit; a broken and a contrite heart, O God, thou wilt not despise.* Psalm 51:17 ESV**

Today, I'm thankful for:

_____
_____
_____
_____
_____
_____
_____
_____

Day 306
Thankful that His name is above every name. At His name, things happen. Try it, call Him!
#forYournamesake

***Therefore God exalted Him to the highest place and gave Him the name that is above every name, that at the name of Jesus every knee should bow, in heaven and on earth and under the earth and every tongue acknowledge that Jesus Christ is Lord, to the glory of God the Father.* Philippians 2:9-11 NIV**

Today, I'm thankful for:

_____
_____
_____
_____
_____
_____
_____
_____

Day 307
Thankful for my positive thoughts overtaking the negative thoughts that sometime creep into my head.
#speaklife
#staypositive

We demolish arguments and every pretension that sets itself up against the knowledge of God, and we take captive every thought to make it obedient to Christ. **2 Corinthians 10:5 NIV**

Today, I'm thankful for:

_____
_____
_____
_____
_____
_____
_____
_____

Day 308
Thankful that the Lord fights my battles! I'm going to let Him do what He does.
#existstageleft
#sittingdownsomewhere

O Lord, oppose those who oppose me. Fight those who fight against me. **Psalm 35:1 NLT**

Today, I'm thankful for:

_____
_____
_____
_____
_____
_____
_____

Day 309
Thankful that the Lord does not forsake His own. No need to beg.
#ItallcomesfromGod

I have been young, and now am old; yet have I not seen the righteous forsaken, nor his seed begging bread. **Psalm 37:25 KJV**

Today, I'm thankful for:

_____
_____
_____
_____
_____
_____
_____
_____

Day 310
Thankful for the supernatural. Yes, it still happens. Believe it!
#Heneverchanges
#Greateriscoming
#doyoubelieve

Verily, verily, I say unto you, He that believeth on me, the works that I do shall he do also; and greater works than theses shall he do; because I go unto my Father. **John 14:12 KJV**

Today, I'm thankful for:

_____
_____
_____
_____
_____
_____
_____
_____

Day 311

Thankful that my God has *no* limits. There are no boundaries with Him!
#Hewilldoitforyoutoo

Great is our Lord and mighty in power; his understanding has no limit. Psalm 147:5 NIV

Today, I'm thankful for:

_____

_____

_____

_____

_____

_____

_____

_____

Day 312

Thankful that it won't always be like this. I have faith that He is going to turn this situation around for my good.
#canyouseechangecoming

So all who put their faith in Christ share the same blessing Abraham received because of his faith. Galatians 3:9 NLT

Today, I'm thankful for:

_____

_____

_____

_____

_____

_____

_____

_____

Day 313

Thankful that He mends broken hearts. He is a heart fixer.
#Heisputtingitbacktogether

The LORD *is close to the brokenhearted; He rescues those whose* spirits are crushed. Psalm 34:18 NLT

Today, I'm thankful for:

_____

_____

_____

_____

_____

_____

_____

_____

Day 314

Thankful that after I have suffered for a little while, He will restore, strengthen, and establish me.
#restoredstrengthenedandestablished

And the God of all grace, who called you to his eternal glory in Christ, after you have suffered a little while, will himself restore you and make you strong, firm and steadfast. 1 Peter 5:10 NIV

Today, I'm thankful for:

_____

_____

_____

_____

_____

_____

_____

_____

Day 315
Thankful that what the enemy meant for bad, God is working it out for my good!
#victorious

You intended to harm me, but God intended it for good to accomplish what is now being done, the saving of many lives. Genesis 50:20 NIV

Today, I'm thankful for:

_____
_____
_____
_____
_____
_____
_____
_____

Day 316
Thankful that He will make a way out of *no* way. Remember the Red Sea? He is the same God!
#Histimingisimpeccable

For I am about to do something new. See, I have already begun! Do you not see it? I will make a pathway through the wilderness. I will create rivers in the dry wasteland. Isaiah 43:19 NLT

Today, I'm thankful for:

_____
_____
_____
_____
_____
_____
_____
_____

Day 317

Thankful that when I seek The Lord with my whole heart, I find Him! #drawneartoHim

But if from there you seek the LORD your God, you will find Him if you seek Him with all your heart and with all your soul.
Deuteronomy 4:29 NIV

Today, I'm thankful for:

_____

_____

_____

_____

_____

_____

_____

_____

Day 318

Thankful that I have been redeemed. Let the redeemed of The Lord say so! #itISso

Has the LORD redeemed you? Then speak out! Tell others he has redeemed you from your enemies. **Psalm 107:2 NLT**

Today, I'm thankful for:

_____

_____

_____

_____

_____

_____

_____

_____

Day 319
Thankful that I don't have to believe the lies of the devil. If he has never told you the truth, why do you keep believing him?
#whatisyourtruth #standonit #heisaliar

You belong to your father, the devil, and you want to carry out your father's desires. He was a murderer from the beginning, not holding to the truth, for there is no truth in him. When he lies, he speaks his native language, for he is a liar and the father of lies. John 8:44 NIV

Today, I'm thankful for:

_____
_____
_____
_____
_____
_____
_____
_____

Day 320
Thankful for the worship of "Oh!" When you can't find the words to say or muster up the strength to even think, give God an "Oh" from the depth of your soul.
#Hehearsyourcry

In my distress I called to the LORD; I cried to my God for help. From his temple He heard my voice; my cry came before Him, into his ears. Psalm 18:6 NIV

Today, I'm thankful for:

_____
_____
_____
_____
_____
_____
_____
_____

Day 321
Thankful for deliverance. Although, I'm not where I ought to be, thank
God I'm not where I used to be!
#nolongerbound
#released

**For you have delivered my soul from death, yes, my feet from falling,
that I may walk before God in the light of life.
Psalm 56:13 ESV**

Today, I'm thankful for:

_____
_____
_____
_____
_____
_____
_____
_____
_____

Day 322
Thankful for His faithfulness. His loving-kindness is immeasurable.
#wordscannotexpress

**Know therefore that the LORD your God, He is God, the faithful
God, who keeps His covenant and His lovingkindness to a
thousandth generation with those who love Him and keep His
commandments; Deuteronomy 7:9 NASB**

Today, I'm thankful for:

_____
_____
_____
_____
_____
_____
_____
_____

Day 323
Thankful that You have given us everything needed to live a godly life.
#keepHiscommandments

His divine power has granted to us all things that pertain to life and godliness, through the knowledge of Him who called us to His own glory and excellence. **2 Peter 1:3 ESV**

Today, I'm thankful for:

_____

_____

_____

_____

_____

_____

_____

_____

Day 324
Thankful that you made us unique with love and care.
#Hiscreationisvast

I praise you because I am fearfully and wonderfully made; your works are wonderful, I know that full well.
Psalm 139:14 NIV

Today, I'm thankful for:

_____

_____

_____

_____

_____

_____

_____

_____

Day 325
Thankful that the Spirit makes intercession on my behalf. Sometimes I just
can't articulate what I need.
#Heknowswhatweneed
#Heismyfilter

**In the same way, the Spirit helps us in our weakness. We do not
know what we ought to pray for, but the Spirit himself intercedes for
us through wordless groans.** Romans 8:26 NIV

Today, I'm thankful for:

_____
_____
_____
_____
_____
_____
_____
_____

Day 326
Thankful that the Lord's way is perfect. Even when things don't go the
way I think they should, I can always count on it to work out for my good.
#Hiswayisperfect
#Hiswillbedoneonearth
#HiswillbedoneinHeaven

**As for God, His way is perfect: The Lord's word is flawless; He
shields all who take refuge in Him.** Psalm 18:30 NIV

Today, I'm thankful for:

_____
_____
_____
_____
_____
_____
_____
_____

Day 327
Thankful for godly counsel. Be careful from whom you receive advice.
#Bewise
#listentogodlyadvice

The way of fools seem right to them, but the wise listen to advice.
Proverbs 12:15 NIV

Today, I'm thankful for:

_____
_____
_____
_____
_____
_____
_____
_____

Day 328
Thankful that I have tasted and seen how good the Lord is. Oh yes, He is!
I want more!
#Mmmm

Taste and see that the Lord is good; blessed is the one who takes
refuge in Him. Psalm 34:8 NIV

Today, I'm thankful for:

_____
_____
_____
_____
_____
_____
_____
_____

Day 329
Thankful for His plans for me. Yes, He loves us just that much!
#receieveHisinstruction

I will instruct you and teach you in the way you should go; I will counsel you with my loving eye on you. **Psalm 32:8 NIV**

Today, I'm thankful for:

_____

_____

_____

_____

_____

_____

_____

_____

Day 330
Thankful that He gives me the strength to keep moving. When I want to give up, He always sends me exactly what I need to press forward.
#weareSTRONGintheLORD
#keepmovingNOmatterwhat

That is why, for Christ's sake, I delight in weaknesses, in insults, in hardships, in persecutions, in difficulties. For when I am weak, then I am strong. **2 Corinthians 12:10 NIV**

Today, I'm thankful for:

_____

_____

_____

_____

_____

_____

_____

_____

Day 331
Thankful that when I am surrounded by darkness, His Word will be my light.
#itisHIDDENinme

Your Word is a lamp to guide my feet and a light for my path.
Psalm 119:105 NLT

Today, I'm thankful for:

_____
_____
_____
_____
_____
_____
_____
_____

Day 332
Thankful for self-control. Be careful of what you say and do to others.
#justbecauseyoucandoesNOTmeanyouhaveto
#controlyourself

A man without self-control is like a city broken into and left without walls. **Proverbs 25:28 ESV**

Today, I'm thankful for:

_____
_____
_____
_____
_____
_____
_____
_____

Day 333
Thankful that He keeps me as the apple of His eye; He hides me from my enemies.
#Hekeepsme
#Hecoversme

Keep me as the apple of your eye; hide me in the shadow of your wings from the wicked who are out to destroy me, from mortal enemies who surround me. Psalm 17:8-9 NIV

Today, I'm thankful for:

_____
_____
_____
_____
_____
_____
_____
_____

Day 334
Thankful that we are allowed the freedom to know Him. Knowing Him provides me with grace and peace in abundance.
#knowledgeisPower
#HisgraceHispeace

Grace and peace be yours in abundance through the knowledge of God and of Jesus our Lord. 2 Peter 1:2 NIV

Today, I'm thankful for:

_____
_____
_____
_____
_____
_____
_____
_____

Day 335
Thankful that He wipes my tears and comforts me. Know that we can
always depend on Him.
#Heisakeeper
#tearsgone

**He will wipe every tear from their eyes. There will be no more death'
or mourning or crying or pain, for the old order of things has passed
away. Revelation 21:4 NIV**

Today, I'm thankful for:

_____
_____
_____
_____
_____
_____
_____
_____
_____

Day 336
Thankful for another day to magnify the Lord and exalt His name.
#glorifytheFather
#IwanttomirrorYou

**Let all that I am praise the LORD. O LORD my God, how great you
are! You are robed with honor and majesty.
Psalm 104:1 NLT**

Today, I'm thankful for:

_____
_____
_____
_____
_____
_____
_____
_____

Day 337
Thankful for silent tears. He is producing *greatness*; just wait and see.
Greater works are coming.
#watchHimwork
#worldchanger

Those who sow in tears shall reap with shouts of joy!
Psalm 126:5 ESV

Today, I'm thankful for:

_____
_____
_____
_____
_____
_____
_____
_____

Day 338
Thankful for my dreams becoming a reality. The Lord, my God, is faithful.
#livingmydreams
#GodisFAITHFUL

Commit to the LORD whatever you do, and He will establish your plans. **Proverbs 16:3 NIV**

Today, I'm thankful for:

_____
_____
_____
_____
_____
_____
_____
_____

Day 339

Thankful that we have already been healed by Jesus' stripes. His action on the cross has made us whole. Die to self and live for righteousness.
#bewhole
#behealed
#befree

"He himself bore our sins" in his body on the cross, so that we might die to sins and live for righteousness; "by his wounds you have been healed." 1 Peter 2:24 NIV

Today, I'm thankful for:

_____
_____
_____
_____
_____
_____
_____
_____

Day 340

Thankful that when I feel closed in, troubled on every side, He makes a way out of no way. He is my deliverer!
#delivered #troubledoesnotlast

He is my loving God and my fortress, my stronghold and my deliverer, my shield, in whom I take refuge, who subdues peoples under me. Psalm 144:2 NIV

Today, I'm thankful for:

_____
_____
_____
_____
_____
_____
_____
_____

Day 341

Thankful for abundant living. The door is open for you to receive. Don't pass the opportunity to truly experience life in abundance.
#acceptHimandlive

I am the door. If anyone enters by me, he will be saved and will go in and out and find pasture. The thief comes only to steal and kill and destroy. I came that they may have life and have it abundantly.
John 10:9-10 ESV

Today, I'm thankful for:

_____
_____
_____
_____
_____
_____
_____
_____

Day 342

Thankful that we win, no matter what. Face every situation and circumstance with a victorious attitude.
#noroomfordefeat
#triumphant

But thanks be to God, who in Christ always leads us in triumphal procession, and through us spreads the fragrance of the knowledge of Him everywhere. **2 Corinthians 2:14 ESV**

Today, I'm thankful for:

_____
_____
_____
_____
_____
_____
_____
_____

Day 343

Thankful that *no* weapon formed against me will prosper. He didn't say that the weapons wouldn't form. But know this: they *won't* prosper! #itwillnotwork #waistedammo

"No weapon that is formed against you will prosper; And every tongue that accuses you in judgment you will condemn. This is the heritage of the servants of the LORD, And their vindication is from Me," declares the LORD. Isaiah 54:17 ESV

Today, I'm thankful for:

_____

_____

_____

_____

_____

_____

_____

_____

Day 344

Thankful that when there is no one in site, no one I can call upon, I can pick up the Word of God and be encouraged. Are you able to encourage yourself in the Word?
#theWordgiveslife #theWordstrengthens

And David was greatly distressed; for the people spake of stoning him, because the soul of all the people was grieved, every man for his sons and for his daughters: but David encouraged himself in the LORD his God. 1 Samuel 30:6 KJV

Today, I'm thankful for:

_____

_____

_____

_____

_____

_____

_____

_____

Day 345

Thankful that I made the choice to trust Jesus. It hasn't been an easy road but, it has been well worth it. I wouldn't trade it for anything in the world. #Heisworthitall
#IcannotlivewithoutHim

Those who know your name trust in you, for you, LORD, have never forsaken those who seek you. Psalm 9:10 NIV

Today, I'm thankful for:

_____

_____

_____

_____

_____

_____

_____

_____

Day 346

Thankful that when I stand in the face of opposition, sometimes I don't even have to say a word. The Father steps right in and handles my accuser. #notmybattle

But the Lord is faithful, and he will strengthen you and protect you from the evil one. 2 Thessalonians 3:3 NIV

Today, I'm thankful for:

_____

_____

_____

_____

_____

_____

_____

Day 347
Thankful that we serve a prayer answering God. We sometimes have to
wait, but it is worth it. #Iamwillingtowait #donotgetweary

**Yet those who wait for the Lord will gain new strength; They will
mount up with wings like eagles, they will run and not get tired, they
will walk and not become weary.   Isaiah 40:31 NASB**

Today, I'm thankful for:

_____
_____
_____
_____
_____
_____
_____
_____

Day 348
Thankful for knowing that if I hold on, my joy will come in the morning.
#peaceinthestorm

**For his anger lasts only a moment, but his favor lasts a lifetime;
weeping may stay for the night, but rejoicing comes in the morning.
Psalm 30:5 NIV**

Today, I'm thankful for:

_____
_____
_____
_____
_____
_____
_____
_____

Day 349

Thankful that even when I have to go through the valley, I'm not alone. I don't have to be afraid.
#comfortmeLord

Even though I walk through the darkest valley, I will fear no evil, for you are with me; your rod and your staff, they comfort me.
Psalm 23:4 NIV

Today, I'm thankful for:

_____

_____

_____

_____

_____

_____

_____

_____

Day 350

Thankful for my daily bread. He gives me exactly what I need for the day. I don't want any more than He desires me to have.
#daybyday
#eattheWord

Give us day by day our daily bread. Luke 11:3 NIV

Today, I'm thankful for:

_____

_____

_____

_____

_____

_____

_____

_____

Day 351
Thankful that You are always in my midst; that you rejoice over me with gladness.
#ThankYouforlovingme

The LORD your God is in your midst, a mighty one who will save; He will rejoice over you with gladness; He will quiet you by his love; He will exult over you with loud singing. Zephaniah 3:17 ESV

Today, I'm thankful for:

_____
_____
_____
_____
_____
_____
_____
_____

Day 352
Thankful for a true relationship with the Father, Son, and the Holy Spirit! This walk can be difficult but with God *all* things are possible.
#itispossiblewithGod

"I am the vine; you are the branches. If you remain in me and I in you, you will bear much fruit; apart from me you can do nothing. John 15:5 NIV

Today, I'm thankful for:

_____
_____
_____
_____
_____
_____
_____
_____

Day 353

Thankful that when God begins a good work in you, He sees it through to the end. He's not finished with me yet!
#LetHimwork

And I am certain that God, who began the good work within you, will continue his work until it is finally finished on the day when Christ Jesus returns. **Philippians 1:6 NLT**

Today, I'm thankful for:

_____
_____
_____
_____
_____
_____
_____
_____

Day 354

Thankful for the sacrifice that You made, Lord. You knew no sin, yet you took on the sins of the world, including mine. Your action allowed us to become filled with the righteousness of God.
#youbecameSIN

God made Him who had no sin to be sin for us, so that in Him we might become the righteousness of God. **2 Corinthians 5:21 NIV**

Today, I'm thankful for:

_____
_____
_____
_____
_____
_____
_____
_____

Day 355
Thankful for a great teacher. I desire your Spirit to lead me at all times.
Help me Lord!
#leadmeandIwillfollow

Teach me to do Your will, for You are my God; may Your good Spirit lead me on level ground. Psalm 143:10 NIV

Today, I'm thankful for:

_____
_____
_____
_____
_____
_____
_____
_____
_____

Day 356
Thankful for *faith*. I can believe it, even when I can't see it. Whether your faith is mountain moving or mustard seed, activate it!
#nomatterhowlargeorsmall

So you see faith by itself isn't enough. Unless it produces good deeds, it is dead and useless. James 2:17 NLT

Today, I'm thankful for:

_____
_____
_____
_____
_____
_____
_____
_____
_____

Day 357
Thankful that I can praise Him without restrictions! How will you praise Him?
#forYournamesake
#Ichoosetoworship

Let them praise his name with dancing and make music to Him with timbrel and harp. **Psalm 149:3 NIV**

Today, I'm thankful for:

_____
_____
_____
_____
_____
_____
_____
_____

Day 358
Thankful that I hear Your voice. It is mighty and majestic. Help me Father, to dispel fear, and move when You speak.
#Hespeakswithauthority

The voice of the LORD is powerful; the voice of the LORD is full of majesty. **Psalm 29:4 ESV**

Today, I'm thankful for:

_____
_____
_____
_____
_____
_____
_____
_____

Day 359
Thankful that He has set a standard for His children. It's not always what we want to do but in the end it's what's *best* for us!
#liveforChrist

Whoever says, "I know Him," but does not do what He commands is a liar, and the truth is not in that person. But if anyone obeys His word, love for God is truly made complete in them. This is how we know we are in Him: Whoever claims to live in Him must live as Jesus did. 1 John 2:4-6 NIV

Today, I'm thankful for:

_____
_____
_____
_____
_____
_____
_____
_____
_____

Day 360
Thankful for the kindness, favor and love that God continues to show me. I praise *Your* name!
#GlorytoYourname

Because Your lovingkindness is better than life, My lips will praise You. Psalm 63:3 NASB

Today, I'm thankful for:

_____
_____
_____
_____
_____
_____
_____
_____

Day 361

Thankful for the woman that I have become. I never imagined this as my life. You have done exceedingly and abundantly above anything I ever dreamed.

#growinginHim

Now all glory to God, who is able, through his mighty power at work within us, to accomplish infinitely more than we might ask or think. **Ephesians 3:20 NLT**

Today, I'm thankful for:

_____

_____

_____

_____

_____

_____

_____

_____

Day 362

Thankful that I no longer have to live depressed and defeated. When I look back over my life, I can see Your perfect fingerprint.

#Yourtouchisreal

The righteous cry out, and the LORD hears them; He delivers them from all their troubles. **Psalm 34:17 NIV**

Today, I'm thankful for:

_____

_____

_____

_____

_____

_____

_____

_____

Day 363
Thankful that when my spirit is downcast, You, oh Lord will lift me up.
#YouhaveNEVERfailedme

Why, my soul, are you downcast? Why so disturbed within me? Put your hope in God, for I will yet praise Him, my Savior and my God.
Psalm 43:5 NIV

Today, I'm thankful for:

_____
_____
_____
_____
_____
_____
_____
_____
_____

Day 364
Thankful that I am being transformed to Your image daily. It can be hard to walk in the Spirit but with You, it is possible.
#witness
#makemenew

And we all, who with unveiled faces contemplate the Lord's glory, are being transformed into His image with ever-increasing glory, which comes from the Lord, who is the Spirit.
2 Corinthians 3:18 NIV

Today, I'm thankful for:

_____
_____
_____
_____
_____
_____
_____
_____
_____

Day 365
Thankful that I try to think before I speak. I now understand the *power* of my words.
#speakpositivealways
#PowerfulWords

The tongue can bring death or life; those who love to talk will reap the consequences. Proverbs 18:21 NLT

Today, I'm thankful for:

_____

_____

_____

_____

_____

_____

_____

_____

No matter what you are going through, I encourage you to search for something to be thankful for each day!

Prayer

You are an awesome God. Mighty in all of Your ways. You are King of kings and Lord of lords. You are worthy of all praise, glory and honor; it all belongs to you. There is no one like you. I love you and I adore you. Father, please forgive me for every wrong thought, action and deed that I have practiced. Cleanse my heart and my mind. It is my desire to turn from my wicked ways and honor You with my daily living. Thank you for the blood You shed on my behalf. I can never repay You. My heart is overwhelmed with gratefulness. Thank you for the reminder that every day I have a reason to be thankful. In Jesus name…Amen.

Made in the USA
Middletown, DE
23 January 2017